PRAISE FOR *WINNING CASE PREPARATION*

"From four of the country's leading thinkers on trial advocacy comes a book that describes a powerful model for preparing a case for trial. The analysis on focus groups is brilliant. I especially like the observation that we should keep asking questions of the focus group members until we understand not just what they think, but also why. This is one of the books that should be read by every lawyer before beginning to prepare a case for trial."

—Mark Mandell, member of the Inner Circle of Advocates, author of *Case Framing*, and past president of the AAJ

"This book offers the reader, whether a lawyer preparing their first case for trial or a seasoned trial lawyer, a methodology grounded in the principles of cognitive science and years of focus-group research. The authors provide readers with the tools to apply an empirical process for constructing a winning trial narrative. I have found the Bottom Up methodology to be the most useful tool I have utilized for preparing a winning case for my clients."

—Kathleen Flynn Peterson, past president of the AAJ, member of the American College of Trial Lawyers and the International Society of Barristers, recipient of ATLA's Lifetime Achievement Award, named one of the top 500 Leading Lawyers in America by *Lawdragon*

"When a courtroom lawyer stops learning, it's time to quit. This work will stand through time in the pantheon of greatest works on human behavior, strategies, and preparation for the trial of individual cases. It is a righteous work which will keep us all learning."

—Russ Herman, past president of the AAJ, past president of the Roscoe Pound Foundation

"I have used Winning Works since 2007. I have seen the principles and science behind Bottom Up case preparation significantly increase the value of my cases. I have completely changed the way I evaluate, litigate, and try cases as their insights have opened my eyes to the real reasons jurors decide the way they do."

—Andrew Abraham, past president of the Massachusetts Academy of Trial Attorneys, listed as a "Rising Star" in *Boston Magazine* and *Super Lawyers* in 2005

"Simply put—*Winning Case Preparation* is a grand slam. This book will take every advocate, from young lawyer to the seasoned veteran, on a journey to maximizing results for their clients. It is about grasping fundamentals, constructing foundations, and mastering strategy and persuasion. Focusing on the realities and necessities of preparation is what every advocate needs. On a 1 to 10 scale, this book is an 11!"

—John Romano, past president of the Academy of Florida Trial Lawyers, the Southern Trial Lawyers Association, and the National Trial Lawyers Association, editor of *Anatomy of a Personal Injury Lawsuit*, 4th edition

"The Overcoming Juror Bias seminars revolutionized the way trial lawyers understand juries and shed light on why good lawyers lose good cases. *Winning Case Preparation: Understanding Jury Bias* goes even further and provides trial lawyers with the tools necessary to identify, understand, and address jurors' preconceived notions of the evidence to achieve justice for our clients. A huge 'thank you' needs to go out to Bossart, Cusimano, Lazarus, and Wenner for sharing their decades worth of knowledge with all of us who exercise the 7th Amendment."

—Tad Thomas, former acting executive director in the Office of Civil and Environmental Law and assistant deputy attorney general for the Office of the Kentucky Attorney General

"The research and analysis the authors present as to the biases that jurors bring with them delivers insights that will fundamentally change how plaintiffs' lawyers prepare and try their cases. To provide the best client representation possible, plaintiffs' lawyers must understand and apply the authors' insights, concepts, and recommendations. This book describes what we need to know about jurors' thinking in a clear and engaging format. Every plaintiffs' lawyer should have this book—and have a highlighter handy when reading it."

—Jerome F. O'Neill, recipient of AAJ's Wiedemann & Wysocki Award, rated AV Preeminent by Martindale-Hubbell

"Written by the top trial strategists and jury consultants of our time, this instructional book is a must-read. *Winning Case Preparation: Understanding Jury Bias* offers a strategic framework and invaluable insight for understanding juror preconceptions and overcoming the hurdles of juror bias to succeed at trial. It's a thoughtful, intuitive, easy-to-read guide that's absolutely necessary for any practitioner who intends to be persuasive in the courtroom."

—Andrew Meyer, achieved one of the highest PI injury awards in Massachusetts history, rated AV Preeminent by Martindale-Hubbell

"From the original visionaries in understanding juror bias comes another great work where method, mapping, and testing in the Bottom Up strategy become synonymous with understanding why and how jurors decide cases. This book is an absolute must-read that's full of practical preparation pointers. It's perfect!"

—Mel C. Orchard, past president of the Wyoming TLA, rated AV Preeminent by Martindale-Hubbell

"It's the Rosetta Stone for translating the facts of your case into a compelling and winning trial story."

—Dan Dell'Osso, obtained one of the top 100 verdicts in the US in 2015, rated AV Preeminent by Martindale-Hubbell

"Finally, a book that distinguishes legal proof from jury proof. This book emphasizes the outcome determinative difference between the two. If I only had three or four books on my shelf, this book would definitely be one of them. *Winning Case Preparation* is based on science, yet it focuses on the perspectives and frames of the human condition."

—William Harper, past president of the Minnesota Association of Justice and recipient of their Lifetime Achievement Award, rated AV Preeminent by Martindale-Hubbell

WINNING CASE PREPARATION

Understanding Jury Bias

DAVID R. BOSSART

GREGORY S. CUSIMANO

EDWARD H. LAZARUS

DAVID A. WENNER

TRIAL GUIDES, LLC

Trial Guides, LLC, Portland, Oregon 97210

ISBN: 978-1-941007-72-3

Library of Congress Control Number: 2018932321

Trial Guides, LLC
Attn: Permissions
2350 NW York Street
Portland, OR 97210
(800) 309-6845
www.trialguides.com

Acquiring Editor: Tina Ricks

Editor: Travis Kremer

Cover Designer: Michael Fofrich

Copyeditor: Patricia Esposito

Proofreader: Tara Lehmann

Original Interior Template Design by Laura Lind Design

Interior Layout by Travis Kremer

Printed and bound in the United States of America.

Printed on acid-free paper.

We dedicate this book to all plaintiffs' trial lawyers, young and old, who have justice in their hearts and a passion to help injured people wronged by the negligence of others, and to all lawyers who are always willing to learn by trying new ideas to help their clients win in front of today's juries.

Contents

ACKNOWLEDGEMENTS

We would be remiss not to thank the great lawyers whom we have had the privilege of working with, observing, and learning from. There are too many to name, and we fear beginning the list would only offend by our errors of omission. But that does not reduce in any way how grateful we are for the honor of our association with you.

We also benefited from the academic work that forms the basis of the Jury Bias Model. As we say over and over again, we did not invent or discover any of the psychological principles on which we base our work. Rather, we tested and applied to the trial setting the well-researched and well-documented findings from the work of academic professionals. Particularly, we want to thank Stanford psychologist Lee Ross for his ongoing generosity with his time and knowledge as Wenner and Cusimano were developing the Jury Bias Model; Cornell psychologist Valerie Hans for her ongoing interest in, support of, and contributions to the model; and researchers for the American Bar Foundation. There are too many other researchers and social scientists whose work we drew upon to mention here.

Other lawyers who also helped with the development of the Jury Bias Model, either through enabling the project or working to adopt the research findings, include Jim Lees, Neal Feigenson, Mark Mandell, Howard Nations, Amato DeLuca, Larry Stewart, Margie Lehrman, and Anjali Jesseramsing. Thanks to Martin Peterson for helping us develop and use "concept" focus groups in a trial setting. There are others as well, whose contributions were valuable.

Diane Lazarus lent her professional time, keen eye, and critical insights to several manuscripts. We all benefited from her contributions and observations. We also all benefited from the patience, understanding, and tolerance of both Alice Cusimano and Bette Bossart.

We gained helpful input from those who commented on a review copy of this book. Not all of their comments were adopted, but we took them all to heart and appreciate the time, energy, and constructive criticisms.

Melanie Jeffcoat and her crew at Circle-X films gave us the gift of their professional time and talent to get our ramblings and approach recorded in a way that became the organizational framework for this book. Janice Pennington took that recording and somehow turned it into a draft.

None of that would have happened, nor would this book exist at all, but for the efforts of Glenn Gutek. Glenn's urging, cajoling, exhorting, encouragement, and organizational skills made this book a reality. We know, because we tried to get started on this book for years before Glenn made it his personal mission to make us focus and do the work of getting it done.

The good people at Trial Guides had to wait a long time for us to get this book written—long enough for us to realize we could not get it done without Glenn, and then longer still once Glenn figured out a way to make us do it. We are grateful to them for not giving up on us, and for keeping us directed toward an ever better final product. We are particularly grateful to Tina Ricks and Travis Kremer for their work in improving this book and seeing it through to the end.

We take full responsibility for the content, along with any errors or omissions it might reveal. But the product itself owes its existence to all of those we acknowledge above.

Publisher's Note

This book is intended for practicing attorneys. It does not offer legal advice or take the place of consultation with an attorney who has appropriate expertise and experience.

Attorneys are strongly cautioned to evaluate the information, ideas, and opinions set forth in this book in light of their own research, experience, and judgment. Readers should also consult applicable rules, regulations, procedures, cases, and statutes (including those issued after the publication date of this book), and make independent decisions about whether and how to apply such information, ideas, and opinions for particular cases.

Quotations from cases, pleadings, discovery, and other sources are for illustrative purposes only and may not be suitable for use in litigation in any particular case.

All individual and business names that appear in illustrative examples have been fictionalized, and any resemblance between these fictional names and real persons is strictly coincidental and unintentional. Real names are used only in reported cases for which citations are given in the footnotes.

All references to the trademarks of third parties are strictly informational and for the purposes of commentary. No sponsorship or endorsement by, or affiliation with, the trademark owners is claimed or implied by the authors or publisher of this book.

The authors and publisher disclaim any liability or responsibility for loss or damages resulting from the use of this book or the information, ideas, and opinions contained in this book.

INTRODUCTION

Why Do Good Lawyers Lose Good Cases?

The facts and the law are important to the outcome of your case, but they are often not as important as the way you pull the facts and law together. Your trial story must be based on what jurors believe and expect. If your story conflicts with jurors' beliefs and expectations, the best facts and strongest case law won't help you. Your case must start with what the jurors believe about your facts and must follow their reasoning to a conclusion that is consistent with what the law calls for as a just outcome.

Law school teaches you to start with the facts. You learn to apply the facts to the law when you prepare a case to meet the requirements of the jury instructions and verdict form. This book presents a departure from the traditional case preparation method. We call it the *Bottom Up*™ approach.[1]

The Bottom Up approach also starts with the facts. But then it centers on how jurors will perceive and interpret those facts. It returns to the facts over and over again to study how you can add,

---

[1] *Bottom Up case preparation* is a term based on research coined by Gregory S. Cusimano and Winning Works, LLC.

1

subtract, or reorder them to have the greatest impact on the decisions jurors will make. This book is an explanation of both the how and the why of preparing your case from the bottom up.

Jurors' Beliefs Matter

You have to learn how the beliefs jurors bring to your case will affect their judgment. That is why we use focus groups (what we will later explain as *concept focus groups*) at the outset—to discover potential jurors' beliefs. But we also recommend, whenever possible, that you test your resulting trial story (which will hopefully be consistent with jurors' beliefs) using a different kind of focus group (a *structured focus group*) prior to its presentation. As we discuss Bottom Up case preparation in the pages that follow, we will make repeated reference to using different kinds of focus groups for different circumstances.

In a perfect world, we would perform focus groups at several different stages throughout the process of preparing a case. However, most cases do not merit that kind of expenditure, and many don't merit the expense of even a single professionally conducted focus group. We encourage the reader to understand that if you learn the lessons of this book about building a case from the bottom up that's focused on jurors' beliefs, you can apply this approach to *any* case.[2] We have successfully applied this approach to cases regardless of their value, whether a commercial tort or other dispute, and whether a jury or a bench trial. Though we write this book from the perspective of a jury trial, it turns out that the things that drive jurors' decision-making also drive judicial decision-making. As it happens, judges are people too.

---

[2] To illustrate this, we use numerous case examples that range from rear-end collisions to medical malpractice.

SAME INFORMATION,
DIFFERENT CONCLUSIONS

Many of us like to believe that there is a single, universal truth waiting to be discovered by those who have all of the necessary facts. We like to think, "If only the jurors are able to understand this set of facts, the conclusion will be obvious and truth and justice shall prevail." There is a certain comfort in believing that if everyone had access to the same information, everyone would agree. Yet the human experience, and the experience of participants in our justice system, proves otherwise.

In reality, different people, all with access to the same information and the same presentation of facts, reach different conclusions. People reach different conclusions about what is *true* because they start from different places. We each have different beliefs that influence how we perceive and assemble new information about the world around us.

Our belief systems begin forming as soon as we become aware, and they continuously develop, providing structures through which we understand the world. But as our belief systems grow, they also become more rigid and less tolerant of competing theories. We are all selective when we interpret and accept new information. We are much more likely to accept as *true* information that fits within our belief systems, and reject as *false* information that does not. Thus, with greater life experience, we become more and more committed to our belief systems and more likely to reject new information that challenges our sense of how we think the world works.

While each of us likely believes there must be some underlying truth in the universe, what each of us perceives that truth to be will not always be the same. What we each accept as true is highly dependent on the belief systems we have developed. And if different people have different beliefs, and if each of us therefore understands the truth a bit differently, how can any of us be sure that what we know to be true is actually true? More important to the trial lawyer, how can we be sure what we perceive to be true is consistent with what jurors will perceive to be true? Simply giving all the jurors access to the same facts won't do the trick.

For instance, consider a malpractice case where a patient was admitted to an outpatient surgical center. The patient was supposed to undergo a short outpatient surgery and return home the same day. During anesthesia, the patient went into cardiac arrest and could not be resuscitated. The plaintiff's anesthesia expert reviewed the case and concluded that the anesthesiologist was negligent in administering the anesthesia. The expert opined that, because of the patient's anatomy, the possibility of an obstruction was foreseeable. Therefore, the anesthesiologist should have protected the airway during the induction.

The expert could well have been right. But focus group participants almost all believed that the patient had an allergic reaction to the anesthesia, leading to the cardiac arrest. Jurors believed one causal explanation while the expert believed another.

The expert did not account for an allergic reaction in his analysis. As a result, this case is unwinnable with this expert, unless the expert frames his opinion around the jurors' beliefs. The jurors' narrative about cause and effect outweighs the expert's opinion. The expert's testimony doesn't matter, even though the expert may be right. If the expert's interpretation of the facts conflicts with the jurors' perception, the jurors' perception wins. The jurors' narrative trumps everything else, including the facts that the expert testifies to and the lawyer presents.

OUR APPROACH

There is no shortage of information on how lawyers can become better communicators, better at persuading jurors, better at arranging the facts of their cases, and better at "connecting with" juries. But most of this work, piled on top of the countless volumes on how to better perform the technical tasks of being a lawyer, misses the mark when it comes to dealing with the reality that jurors come into the courtroom with different beliefs and life experiences that cause them to react differently to the same information.

The authors of this book approach this problem by following aspects of the scientific method. Rather than putting together an approach based solely on instinct, intuition, and anecdotal experience, we have based Bottom Up case preparation on research in the areas of psychology, social science, cognition, decision-making, persuasion, and communication. We do not offer our *sense* of what works in a trial setting. We present a framework for how to systematically approach trial preparation (including preparation for settlement, arbitration, or mediation) in a way that takes advantage of scientific research findings that can help you better understand how jurors make decisions.

At the heart of our approach is the conviction that there is no magic formula or incantation. While some popular approaches to trial preparation suggest there is one way to present every case, regardless of the facts and circumstances, we believe each case is unique. Our approach applies a systematic method based on the sciences to discover what will work best in each case.

THE ORIGIN OF
BOTTOM UP CASE PREPARATION

Winning Works is a research-based trial consulting firm. We, the principals of Winning Works, have decades of experience in developing persuasive messages that move opinion across a variety of settings. In addition to being accomplished litigators, Greg Cusimano, David Wenner, and David Bossart are nationally recognized experts on the psychological biases and motivations that individuals bring to their assessments of facts. Cusimano and Wenner created the Association of Trial Lawyers of America's® (ATLA®) groundbreaking Overcoming Juror Bias (OJB) education programs. Bossart, Cusimano, and Wenner have been principal contributors to the OJB program's further development since its inception.[3]

Edward Lazarus spent close to a dozen years as one of the nation's leading Democratic political pollsters and campaign strategists. After moving on to expand his work beyond the candidate realm, Lazarus (in addition to advising many political and public relations clients) worked as a consultant to ATLA as well as to roughly two dozen state bar associations and several state courts. During that work, he compiled the largest-known database on public attitudes toward the civil justice system.

In the early 1990s, Cusimano and Wenner (along with others) were concerned with why good lawyers were losing good cases. ATLA tried to address this problem by creating a blue-ribbon committee that Cusimano initially chaired and Wenner later co-chaired, and in which Bossart was very active.

---

[3] The Association of Trial Lawyers of America adopted a new name, the American Association for Justice® (AAJ®), in 2007. We refer to the organization as ATLA because the work being referenced occurred when it was called the Association of Trial Lawyers of America.

At an ATLA CLE program on focus groups in 1994, more than thirty trial lawyers from around the country attended and analyzed more than sixty focus groups. Clear patterns emerged on how the focus-group respondents were processing information. This research, conducted in a scope and volume impossible for any individual trial lawyer or consultant to achieve, led to further examination of the academic literature. The goal was not to be able to report anecdotes about individual trial experiences or focus-group findings, but to develop generalizable theories of juror behavior based in social science, particularly in cognitive and social psychology, relying heavily on Wenner's background in psychology. The theories that emerged were the foundational hypotheses that formed the Jury Bias Model™.

Later, when Lazarus was working in-house at ATLA to coordinate political and legislative efforts and strategies, Cusimano, Wenner, and Bossart discovered that their work and Lazarus's led to the *same substantive conclusions about the art and science of persuading jurors.* Thus, Winning Works was born. Since the creation of Winning Works in 2005, the authors have been involved in some of the largest plaintiffs' verdicts in the country, totaling more than $4 billion.

THE JURY BIAS MODEL

Before Wenner and Cusimano joined with Bossart and Lazarus to create Winning Works and Bottom Up case preparation, they tested the hypotheses of the Jury Bias Model in hundreds of focus groups across the country. They analyzed and honed the model, until they finally defined the five biases that often work against plaintiffs:

1. *Suspicion*: Jurors are suspicious of everyone in the court-room, but particularly of the plaintiff, the plaintiff's attorney, and the plaintiff's claims.
2. *Victimization*: Jurors are worried that they or others will somehow be victimized by the outcome of the trial.
3. *Personal Responsibility*: Jurors are not going to hold a defendant responsible if they feel the plaintiff has behaved irresponsibly.
4. *Stuff Happens*: As the facts or circumstances of the claim become more complicated, it becomes easier and more likely for jurors simply to write off an act of negligence that caused very real harm to the plaintiff as one of those unfortunate things that happen in life.
5. *Blame the Plaintiff*: Jurors tend to overemphasize the plaintiff's role in what went wrong, even in cases where there is a clear pattern of misconduct on the part of the defendant that led to the plaintiff's injury.

THE NEED FOR
BOTTOM UP CASE PREPARATION

Many lawyers still prepare in a largely intuitive way, relying on their training and knowledge of the law, as well as the objective *truth* as defined by fact witnesses, expert witnesses, and the rules of law that apply to their case. They will argue that the defendant had a duty to the plaintiff or the public, the defendant then breached that duty, and a compensable harm resulted.

We encounter far too many instances where an attorney is so confident that the science, the medicine, or the engineering make the defendant's liability so abundantly clear that the lawyer fails to consider how the biases jurors bring into the courtroom might derail the case. Perversely, the stronger lawyers think their case is, the harder it is to force themselves to take the necessary time to consider the impact of juror bias.

As we have previously discussed, jurors do not necessarily make up their minds based on the rules of law or the fact pattern as presented by the attorneys on both sides. Jurors make up their minds based on what makes sense to them, according to their own beliefs and life experiences. No matter how good you are at following the law, it is the jury (most of whom have no experience with the law or the rules of evidence) who get to decide the outcome of your case. Unlike you, the attorney, who has had anywhere from many months to several years to become deeply immersed in the case (during which time you inevitably lose your sense of objectivity), jurors come to the case fresh, with far less knowledge. Their decisions will be made much more on how things appear to them at first rather than how things appear to you after months or years of familiarity.

Doesn't it make sense, therefore, to build your case around the jurors' reality rather than around your reality? If the trial were a commercial marketing effort, the jurors would be the end consumers who decide whether to buy your product or your competitor's. If the trial were a political campaign, the jurors would be the voters who decide to vote for your client or for the opposition. In both of these contexts, the communications effort (the marketing campaign or the political campaign) is designed around how the product or candidate best meets the needs, goals, and expectations of the consumer or voter. Such campaigns are not based on the technical aspects of manufacturing a product or mounting an effort to be elected. Yet many lawyers still focus their case preparation almost exclusively on managing the technical side of their cases, with little or no consideration of jurors' unique perspectives.

Any business has a host of technical components. But mastery of the technical components does not matter if consumers do not buy the product. The business will fail. To the trial lawyer, the jurors are the consumers. If jurors do not believe in your product, you will fail.

Consider the business of running a restaurant. A lot of behind-the-scenes effort goes into making a restaurant work. The owner has to worry (among other things) about creating a menu, designing a dining room, equipping a kitchen, sourcing quality food reliably and affordably, and staffing the kitchen and dining room professionally. But in the end, the business will fail, regardless of how well all of the technical, unseen aspects of the restaurant are run, if the customers say the food is no good. You cannot operate a successful restaurant without worrying about whether diners will enjoy the food.

Similarly, you cannot hope to be consistently successful at trial without holding paramount the concern over how the jurors will accept the case. You cannot rely exclusively on good law, good facts, and good evidence. You have to understand how the evidence and its presentation will strike the jurors.

A similar dynamic exists in the political realm. Any quality candidate has a host of policy goals, but spends time learning which of those goals best captures the imagination and will of the voters. The policy goals and issue positions of the candidates in a political campaign are akin to the facts surrounding a case. Just as political operatives must master the issues and issue positions in a political campaign, you must know the facts as you develop a strategy. But knowing the facts of a case backward and forward isn't enough—any more than knowing the issues is enough to win an election. Knowing how to order the facts, which ones to emphasize and which to de-emphasize in order to most persuasively put together your trial story, is similar to knowing how to talk about the issues and frame the debate in the most favorable light during the course of a political campaign. In political campaigns, focus groups and surveys give the voters a seat at the table so their views can inform the candidate's narrative.

With the Bottom Up approach, you will give the jurors not just a seat at the table but a foundational role in how you build the case and the trial story. You will approach your cases from the bottom up. You will learn the case's facts but never entirely leave them; instead, you will research how jurors are likely to react to those facts, and reframe and resequence them if necessary. This enables you to build the core of the case—your understanding of what is important to potential jurors and what you need to show to win your case.

These elements go into developing your trial story. You won't assume it is right the first time you put it together. You will test and modify your case core and trial story with further jury research, enabling you to learn from mock jurors how close you are to presenting your case in a way that fits into the worldview of a random cross section of people with no prior knowledge of the case.

You will structure the story and layer it in such a way that it fits within the belief systems of those who are naturally plaintiff-friendly as well as those who are naturally hostile toward plaintiffs and the kind of claim that underlies the case. Only after that juror-centric process is complete will you go back and begin the process you learned in law school—applying the law to the case and understanding how the evidence works its way into the narrative.

The Bottom Up approach makes cases more winnable because it structures cases to best communicate the information that is most important to those who decide the case—the jurors. Our effort is designed to take full advantage of the science behind the Jury Bias Model by focusing on the elements of proof that are important to the jury. You still need to prove your case legally, but you also need to prove it to the jury.[4]

---

[4] For further discussion on the differences between proving your case legally versus proving it to the jury, *see* chapter 4, "Investigating the Facts."

For a dramatic example of the limits you face when relying on just the facts and the evidence to win the day without considering the jurors' belief systems, let's return for a moment to the scientific method. It consists of the following steps:

1. Question
2. Research
3. Hypothesize
4. Test
5. Analyze
6. Conclude

Now consider the following: There remains very little doubt within the scientific community that climate change is occurring and that human activity is a contributing factor. Even ExxonMobil acknowledges that human activity, particularly related to the energy industry, has led to an increase in greenhouse gases and resultant climate change.[5]

Yet despite the scientific evidence, and the agreement of the world's largest corporation (which would seem to have a larger vested interest than any other entity on the planet in denying the reality of climate change and its human component), vast numbers of Americans deny that climate change is occurring or, if it is, that human activity is in any way related. In other words, here is an issue that science tells us is of major social importance on a global scale, yet one-third of Americans believe the problem does not exist at all, and roughly half believe that to the extent the problem exists, human behavior has nothing to do with it.[6]

---

[5] *See* "Our Position on Climate Change," ExxonMobil Corporation, last accessed June 7, 2017, www.corporate.exxonmobil.com/en/current-issues/climate-policy/climate-perspectives/our-position.

[6] Cary Funk and Brian Kennedy, *The Politics of Climate* (Washington, DC: The Pew Research Center, 2016), www.pewinternet.org/2016/10/04/the-politics-of-climate/.

The same process that demonstrates the reality of climate change (the scientific method) also allows us to understand how, and why, so many Americans (potential jurors) deny climate science. Psychological principles discovered through the scientific method enlighten our understanding of those who don't believe in climate change. Climate science does not fit within their worldview. The same principles of the scientific method enlighten the Jury Bias Model. Bottom Up case preparation is nothing more than following the scientific method:

1. Question the case.
2. Research the facts.
3. Form hypotheses about your case.
4. Test the hypotheses with research.
5. Analyze the results.
6. Use those results as your trial story.

Ironically, one can appropriately call the scientific method itself a belief system, even though adherence to the scientific method requires one to be agnostic about beliefs. Essential to the scientific method is accepting that whatever the data show is what the data show, regardless of any beliefs one carries into the process. Still, those whose belief systems allow no room for climate change or evolution will likely reject the science on which the Jury Bias Model rests, because they simply do not believe in the scientific method.

Chapters 1 and 2 provide an in-depth discussion of the Jury Bias Model, its five biases, and its ten commandments designed to combat or use the biases. Chapter 3 contrasts Bottom Up case preparation to top-down case preparation. The remaining chapters will then discuss each of the elements of Bottom Up case preparation:

- Investigating the Facts
- Conducting Jury Research
- Building the Case Core
- Developing the Trial Story
- Testing Your Case
- Understanding and Applying Beliefs

In the end, we dedicate a final chapter to listening. Listening is a vital, though often woefully undeveloped, skill every lawyer needs to properly prepare for trial. From what your client says to what your focus groups tell you, from what voir dire reveals to what your opposing counsel discloses when presenting their case, listening is an underutilized skill that, when honed, brings great value to your case.

We hope you enjoy this book and find its contents useful in preparing your cases. We have found the structure that follows to be of great use in helping our clients become more successful at what they do. Beyond that, we hope you will find, as we have, that the skills enumerated in this book are helpful far beyond the practice of law. Good communication in any context requires knowing something about your audience. At its heart, Bottom Up preparation is the art and science of learning about your audience—their beliefs, hopes, and expectations—so you can more effectively communicate with them.

1

THE JURY BIAS MODEL
PART ONE
The Five Juror Biases

As you've probably noticed from the introduction, we're obsessed with science. It's what the Jury Bias Model and Bottom Up case preparation are founded on. We'll tell you stories to illustrate a point, but the basis for our method is scientific research, not anecdotal evidence. Everything we do is based on applying tested psychological principles to the field of trial law. When we began, many of the principles we drew on were not new to social scientists; what was different was our conscious decision to apply those principles to combat jury bias as it emerged in the 1980s and 1990s. To our knowledge, no one had applied what psychologists were learning about heuristics or emotional and cognitive biases to the practice of law and the persuasion and influence of jurors.[1] This early research for ATLA opened the door for a host of talented trial lawyers to begin approaching

---

[1] For more on heuristics, *see* the discussion on page 31.

the development of their cases in an entirely new way—based on science rather than on intuition alone.

DEVELOPING THE JURY BIAS MODEL

Wenner has been studying juries since 1979. His research has focused on how jurors process evidence and how that evidence unconsciously impacts their judgment and decision-making.

Before becoming a lawyer, Wenner received a master's in social work and performed individual and group psychotherapy. One of his areas of expertise was hypnotherapy, a practice he learned during his study with the groundbreaking psychologist and hypnotherapist Milton H. Erickson. The father of one of Wenner's patients at the time was a lawyer interested in borrowing from the hypnotherapy strategies that Wenner employed in his therapy practice to use for jury selection at trial. Wenner became so interested in studying jurors' decision-making that he published an article on the subject in *Trial Diplomacy Journal*.[2] Ultimately, he left his private practice and attended law school, intent on integrating his formal training in law and psychology.

Cusimano's path to the study of juror bias was a little different. By the early 1990s, he had tried 150 to 200 cases to verdict. Although Cusimano had studied many of the psychological principles relevant to decision-making as an undergraduate in marketing research, sales, and advertising, his law school professors had told him (mistakenly) to forget all that. Back then, Cusimano's only focus groups were live juries.

---

[2] David Wenner and S. L. Swanson, "Sensory Language in the Courtroom," *Trial Diplomacy Journal* (Winter 1981): 13.

When Cusimano met Wenner, Wenner was working with Martin Peterson, a longtime trial consultant with a PhD in human biology and a master's in anthropology. The pair watched one of Cusimano's closing arguments. Afterward, they commented on Cusimano's effective use of heuristics, like the norm bias and belief perseverance. Cusimano replied, "Don't tell me that—I'm not aware I'm using heuristics, whatever that is. Because if I think about it, I can't do it. And I don't need to think about it." But Cusimano was fascinated, and he's been thinking about it and studying decision science ever since.

As we mentioned in the introduction, Wenner and Cusimano started the first focus group college convened by ATLA's National College of Advocacy (NCA) in Charleston, South Carolina, in 1994. More than thirty trial lawyers brought cases and participated in sixty focus groups involving several hundred people. On the final day of the college, when the faculty and attendees analyzed results from the various focus groups, they discovered similarities in the negative attitudes concerning plaintiffs' purported responsibility for their own injuries. The following year, Wenner and Cusimano led the NCA's second focus group college in Houston, Texas. The results in 1995 were identical to those in 1994. The anti-plaintiff bias was undeniable.

"How bad was jury bias?" Cusimano and Wenner wondered. In April 1995, Larry Stewart, then president of ATLA, appointed Cusimano to chair a blue-ribbon committee of trial lawyers to find out. A number of trial lawyers from around the country attended the first meeting in Atlanta. It quickly became apparent that Wenner was the only other lawyer who shared Cusimano's interest and commitment to the endeavor, so the two effectively became co-chairs of the committee.

Cusimano and Wenner conducted their research the way any scientists would. Over several years, they experimented with hundreds of different focus groups. In addition, they continued to explore, test, and confirm their ideas and findings with other trial lawyers as they taught regularly at ATLA's focus group college, the Case Workshop, and at OJB programs.

To understand the psychological underpinnings of the behaviors they were observing, Cusimano and Wenner conducted an exhaustive review of the academic literature in several fields of the social sciences. They went straight to the leading scholars and thought leaders in the fields of law, psychology, neuroscience, cognition, decision-making, persuasion, and communication to learn all they could about the psychological principles underlying the anti-plaintiff biases they had uncovered.

They consulted with Geoffrey Garin, the president of Hart Research Associates, one of the nation's leading survey research firms. They reviewed much of the research Lazarus carried out during his service with ATLA. They met with Neal Feigenson, a lawyer who spoke at one of ATLA's earliest OJB programs and was interested in some of the same issues Cusimano and Wenner were studying. In his book *Legal Blame*, Feigenson relied on some of Wenner and Cusimano's research with focus groups to analyze how jurors make decisions.[3]

They began a dialogue with Dr. Valerie Hans,[4] one of the nation's leading authorities on social science and the law. Trained as a social scientist, Dr. Hans also used Wenner and Cusimano's focus-group research in a law review article concerning jury decision-making.[5] They also worked with Dr. Stephen Daniels, a senior research professor at the American Bar Foundation, and with Joanne Martin, a senior research fellow in liaison research, also with the American Bar Foundation.

---

[3] Neal Feigenson, *Legal Blame: How Jurors Think and Talk About Accidents* (Washington, DC: American Psychological Association, 2001).

[4] Dr. Hans is presently a professor at Cornell Law School. She is the author or editor of eight books and over a hundred research articles, many of which focus on juries and jury reforms as well as the uses of social science in law.

[5] Valerie P. Hans, "The Contested Role of the Civil Jury in Business Litigation," *Judicature* 79, no. 5 (March–April 1996): 242–248.

However, things began to click into place when Wenner, and later Cusimano, began working with Stanford psychologist Dr. Lee Ross, a pioneer in research on human inference. Years earlier, Ross had published a book on human inference[6] that focused attention on the social psychological research of Daniel Kahneman and Amos Tversky. When Wenner read Ross's book, he quickly realized that Kahneman's[7] and Tversky's work had big implications for trial practice in general, and his and Cusimano's research in particular.

Out of this, Wenner and Cusimano created the Jury Bias Model, providing trial lawyers with a process for analyzing cases and determining their strengths and deficiencies. The Model is founded on psychological principles identified in peer-reviewed research, the sort that could withstand the most withering *Daubert* challenge. Cusimano and Wenner discovered what biases trial lawyers should be wary of and then armed them with tools to combat those biases. Their conclusions were not based on their own experiences or intuitions, but on thousands of hours of painstaking, independent experimentation and research.

The first part of the Jury Bias Model identifies five recurring attitudes that most often negatively influence the public's perception of plaintiffs. Those biases, as mentioned in the introduction to this book, are as follows:[8]

1. Suspicion
2. Victimization

---

[6] Richard E. Nisbett and Lee Ross, *Human Inference: Strategies and Shortcomings of Social Judgment* (Englewood Cliffs, NJ: Prentice-Hall, 1980).

[7] In 2002, Kahneman received the Nobel Prize for his contributions to the field of Economic Sciences. In 2011, *Foreign Policy* magazine named Kahneman to its list of top global thinkers. His book *Thinking, Fast and Slow* was a *New York Times* bestseller. In 2015, *The Economist* listed Kahneman as the seventh most influential economist in the world.

[8] *See* "Introduction," page 8.

3. Personal Responsibility
4. Stuff Happens
5. Blame the Plaintiff

In the second part of the model, Cusimano and Wenner assembled a list of counteractive measures to those biases—psychological principles to incorporate in trial preparation and in trial. Called the *Ten Commandments of the Jury Bias Model*, Wenner and Cusimano tested these principles in hundreds of additional focus groups to ensure their efficacy in case preparation and in trial to help trial lawyers overcome jury bias.

THE FIVE JUROR BIASES

The first part of the Jury Bias Model is based on Cusimano and Wenner's observations during their focus-group research for ATLA. Particularly, they noticed that jurors had similar anti-plaintiff attitudes that had developed largely because of the public barrage of tort reform rhetoric over several decades. Most of these biases are not naturally occurring psychological phenomena, like Monday-morning quarterbacking or loss aversion. Tort reformers have taught the public these anti-plaintiff and anti-plaintiff's lawyer biases. Corporate defendants, Republican strategists, the Manhattan Institute, the American Tort Reform Association (ATRA), the Chamber of Commerce—all have succeeded over the last thirty years in portraying trial attorneys as greedy lawyers who manipulate the courts to line their own pockets at the cost of ordinary consumers.[9] Jurors have heard the rhetoric so long and from so many sources that tort reform slander has worked its way into their belief systems.

---

[9] Stephen Daniels and Joanne Martin, *Tort Reform, Plaintiffs' Lawyers, and Access to Justice* (Lawrence, Kansas: University Press of Kansas, 2015), 3.

Why the vicious attacks? Several reasons. Plaintiffs' lawyers provide access to the legal system for people who could not otherwise afford a lawyer.[10] In addition, they influence the development of liability law by advancing and honing new legal theories for holding accountable those whose negligence has harmed others.[11] Trial lawyers further help to establish the "going rate" that injuries are worth—the amount that a jury would be likely to award at trial.[12] Without trial lawyers, laws protecting ordinary people would never develop and consumers would remain uncompensated, or undercompensated, for their injuries. For organizations like the Chamber of Commerce, that's the goal.

To that end, tort reform proponents have worked diligently and systematically to shape the public mind and the cultural environment concerning civil litigation.[13] One aspect of this campaign is to prejudice the minds of potential jurors long before they ever receive a summons for jury duty.[14] Another is to discourage lawsuits in the first place by persuading the public more broadly that each of us must assume personal responsibility for the misfortunes we suffer.[15] "Stuff happens." As part of this effort, tort reformers have, for decades, used radio, television, billboards, and now internet marketing campaigns to convince the public that everyone is threatened by personal injury litigation because we all must pay higher prices to cover the cost of sizeable jury verdicts.[16] Lawsuits, tort reformers claim, lead to victimization of the public.

---

[10] *Id.* at 10.

[11] *Id.* at 8–11.

[12] *Id.* at 14–15.

[13] *Id.* at 20.

[14] *Id.* at 21.

[15] *Id.* at 22.

[16] *Id.* at 22–26.

During their early work for ATLA, Cusimano and Wenner conducted their own research to tackle the problem. Through focus groups, case workshops, and hundreds of interviews with trial lawyers all over the country, they labored to identify and catalog jurors' deleterious beliefs. They learned that tort reformers had been highly successful in either creating or exploiting five recurring anti-plaintiff attitudes. These biases often caused plaintiffs to lose at trial, though the lawyers trying the cases didn't know why. At the start, Cusimano and Wenner referred to the biases as *untried issues*. The biases were there in the courtroom whether the trial lawyer recognized them or not. Calling them what they were—untried issues—served to motivate trial lawyers to address the biases when they arose. Here, we explore each of the five anti-plaintiff biases trial lawyers must still identify and defuse today.

BIAS ONE: SUSPICION

During their research, Wenner and Cusimano observed that focus-group respondents were filled with *suspicion* from the outset—particularly toward the plaintiff, her attorney, and her claims in the lawsuit. Roughly 80 percent of their focus-group members believed there were too many lawsuits, and 68 percent felt that lawyers encourage plaintiffs to file unnecessary lawsuits.

Their findings are consistent with other researchers' observations: only a third of jurors believe most plaintiffs have legitimate claims.[17] Yet jurors do not harbor the same suspicion of defendants and do not scrutinize their actions as rigorously as they do plaintiffs' conduct.[18] The suspicion bias puts you in the position

---

[17] Valerie P. Hans, "The Contested Role of the Civil Jury in Business Litigation," *Judicature* 79, no. 5 (March–April 1996): 242–248, 244.

[18] *Id.*

of a sales representative on a used-car lot; you know the people you're trying to persuade come through the door with little or no trust in what you say. Although it's not as intense, jurors tend to be suspicious of all lawyers and the judicial system in general.

The Jury Bias Model encourages you to research whether some aspect of the plaintiff's conduct raises jurors' suspicions, causing them to mistrust your client and the case. Be careful, however, as invoking this negative tort reform frame sometimes reinforces it. Applying this negative frame to your case preparation can keep you vigilant about watching for potentially suspicious behaviors from the plaintiff, but it can also cause you to over-focus on defending the detrimental aspects of the plaintiff's conduct.

The better solution is to create a positive frame that helps you focus on building a stronger case, rather than defending against the worst case. Suspicion can be reframed as credibility by identifying conduct that establishes the plaintiff's trustworthiness and by presenting her as a protagonist and witness to the story's events.

A case in which Bossart debriefed the jury for a friend illustrates the debilitating effect of juror suspicion. The lone plaintiff in the wrongful death case was the adult daughter of a sixty-two-year-old man. Everything went so well at trial that the lawyer thought victory was assured. That was prior to the defense verdict.

Bossart was fortunate to be able to review the issues with all six jurors at the same time. After discussing a number of issues, Bossart inquired, "Was there ever a turning point in the trial?" Every single juror smiled. "Okay, somebody say something," Bossart pushed.

"Well, yes," said the foreperson. "The tide turned when the plaintiff got on the witness stand. Just before she started to testify, she pulled the Kleenex box over to her."

Bossart played dumb. "What are you telling me?"

The foreperson replied, "Well, she was getting ready to cry for us."

That's the suspicion bias at work. The plaintiff lost her case because the jurors were so suspicious they doubted her sincere grief over the loss of her father.

Certain types of cases, such as slip and fall and minor impact, heighten juror suspicion, particularly when the plaintiff did not see a doctor or call the police immediately after the incident that caused the injuries. In one of Bossart's own cases, a pickup truck rear-ended his client late one night in what the client thought was a minor crash. The plaintiff exchanged phone numbers with the other driver, but he didn't call the police. That made the jurors suspicious. People assume that if you don't call the police, you're not really injured.

Adding to the jurors' suspicion in Bossart's case was the fact that the plaintiff did not immediately seek medical attention. He waited until the next day when he realized he was really hurt. This is another red flag for jurors. Suspicious jurors will assume that if the plaintiff didn't go to the doctor immediately, he must not have been hurt very badly.

Other suspicions are more pernicious. Focus-group partici-pants always ask, "When did the plaintiff contact the lawyer?" Here, you're trapped between Scylla and Charybdis. If the plain-tiff called her attorney the day after she was injured, jurors are suspicious that her first thought was "jackpot justice." But if she waited eighteen months to contact a lawyer, jurors assume that a friend must have told her that she could turn that old injury into an underserved windfall. Any possible answer to this question creates suspicion.

These issues—whether the plaintiff called the police or when she sought medical attention—are not determinative of the defendant's liability or the plaintiff's injuries. But psychologically, they can be pivotal. When you have an issue like this in your case, prepare to alleviate jurors' suspicion by presenting the plaintiff as a responsible person in all aspects of her life. Distinguish your client from the jackpot-justice prototype jurors envision so that, during deliberation, someone volunteers: "I don't think Jane is the kind of person who would make something up." Distinguish yourself from the prototype people have about trial lawyers who bring frivolous lawsuits.

To be believable, the plaintiff's story must be consistent with jurors' life experiences. Is the plaintiff a credible witness? Are her verbal and nonverbal behaviors congruent? The plaintiff must appear to be open-minded and personally responsible. You have to show that she accepts the consequences of her injuries, especially in instances where jurors are likely to assign her blame. Present the plaintiff as someone who, even in her injured condition, continued to apply for work and asked her doctor to release her for work. Determine if there is something in the plaintiff's background that screams of her good character and honesty. Does she work with the underprivileged? Has she ever found a wallet full of money and turned it in to the lost-and-found? Get the idea? Even having your client admit to something on the stand that doesn't work to her benefit can reflect credibility and responsibility.

All jurors possess an intuitive sense of fairness. They must *feel* that holding the defendant accountable is fair. Jurors measure their perceptions of the fairness of the plaintiff's demand for justice against their views of the wrongfulness of the defendant's conduct and the harmfulness of that conduct to the plaintiff. Jurors want to feel the plaintiff *truly deserves* and needs help.

The more jurors like the plaintiff, the more they are inclined to help her. Simple guidelines should inform the plaintiff's conduct in the courtroom. For instance, people who smile are more likeable than people who frown, so having the plaintiff smile when introduced to the jury for the first time is socially appropriate and encourages jurors to like her.

The bottom line: focus on presenting the plaintiff as a credible, likeable witness to create a positive, hopeful frame that effectively eliminates suspicion.

BIAS TWO: VICTIMIZATION

Victimization is the second juror bias that Cusimano and Wenner identified in their research. People have been conditioned to believe that they, their families, and their communities will somehow be victimized by plaintiffs' personal injury lawsuits. They worry that large verdicts will increase their personal insurance rates, that verdicts against medical professionals will reduce the availability of local health care, or that the cost of their household products or medications will rise. Jurors fear that compensating the plaintiff will bring them harm.

Victimization, the tort-reformer's frame, looks like this: Rewarding the plaintiff only encourages people to be irresponsible and blame their problems on someone else. This leads ultimately to an unsafe world with no accountability. A defense verdict, by contrast, maintains a safe world in which people agree to watch out for themselves.

Some people will think the plaintiff is acting like things "just happened" to her and she had no control over any of it. That's scary and not what some jurors want to believe. Further, jurors want to believe people will "make do and get through" or "get over it" and go on with their lives. Many jurors will resent it if they think you are painting your client as a "victim."

Don't put your client's picture in the victim frame. Reframe the case: The plaintiff is a responsible person who will make do no matter what. It was the single act of this particular defendant that caused the harm, and the defendant should be accountable. By focusing on the defendant alone and his aberrant misconduct, jurors need not worry that a large verdict will encourage more lawsuits. Show jurors that a sizable award in your client's lawsuit will not raise their insurance rates or the cost of their products because this case is the exception, not the rule. Demonstrate that if jurors don't hold the defendant accountable, the world they thought was safe will become a little more dangerous.[19]

BIAS THREE: PERSONAL RESPONSIBILITY

Americans believe strongly in the value of *personal responsibility*.[20] Many see the world as rewarding those who are personally responsible and punishing those who are not. As applied to plaintiffs, this means that injured people get what they deserve. Or that if only the plaintiff had acted responsibly, he would not need a handout from the hardworking defendant. That's the personal-responsibility bias. Cusimano and Wenner saw this over and over in focus-group respondents, concluding that personal responsibility was revered in all demographics. For juries, it is easier to side with plaintiffs who seem personally responsible (people who would, therefore, not file a lawsuit just for the money) than with those who do not.

Wenner and Cusimano observed that focus-group members tended to initially assume that the plaintiff had not behaved responsibly. Jurors often conclude that they would have been more responsible than the plaintiff had been and would have avoided the damage. In general, people tend to overestimate their own abilities and what they would do when compared to others. When they do so, they tend to blame others for being irresponsible.[21]

This assumption leads jurors to impose responsibility for the plaintiff's injuries on the plaintiff rather than the defendant.

---

[19] For a discussion on how to use loss framing to combat the victimization bias, *see* chapter 2, page 56.

[20] Andrew J. Cherlin, "I'm O.K., You're Selfish," *New York Times Magazine*, October 17, 1999.

[21] This is often referred to as the Lake Wobegon Effect. Lake Wobegon appeared in Garrison Keillor's radio series *A Prairie Home Companion*, where "all the children are above average."

Jurors will not hold the defendant accountable unless you first establish that the plaintiff is a responsible person. What's more, jurors hold the plaintiff to a higher standard of personal responsibility than the defendant. This is especially true when the plaintiff is a person and the defendant is a company.

People know how other people should behave, but they may not be sure how a corporation should act. In voir dire and opening statement, you need to explain how the concept of personal responsibility applies to corporations. If you don't do it then, it will never happen—the jury will not make that connection for a corporation.

Counteract the personal-responsibility bias just as you would the suspicion bias or the victimization bias. The plaintiff must be über-responsible—in her family, work, and community. In your case preparation, develop concrete examples of each, including the plaintiff's personal responsibility even in the wake of incredible adversity. Reclaim the moral high ground. Otherwise, the personal-responsibility bias will work against your clients in virtually every case.

For example, we had one case where the plaintiff, Mike Sherman, was on his Harley motorcycle when a pickup truck made a left turn in front of him. He was unable to stop and hit the side of the truck. The pickup truck driver said Mike had to have been speeding around the curve in the road because he hadn't seen him. At that time of day, the sun would have been in the truck driver's eyes, but he claimed he would have been able to see Mike if Mike hadn't been speeding. Mike suffered a traumatic amputation of his foot in the crash.

Focus-group participants initially seemed to think Mike was a stereotypical biker and tended to blame him for his own injuries. Then we fleshed out the facts revealing Mike's character. Once we explained that Mike was a district manager for a telephone company who rode only on the weekends to get out of doors and away from the suit and tie he wore to work, the participants' views generally changed.

However, when the participants learned Mike was a soldier who was decorated for carrying a fellow marine to safety for a quarter mile after an IED exploded, they completely shifted for the plaintiff. They believed him when he said he was traveling below the speed limit and was on his way home. His personal responsibility and apparent bravery carried the day and his case.

BIAS FOUR: STUFF HAPPENS

Stuff happens is the fourth juror bias. In many cases, people are likely to assume that no one was at fault and shrug their shoulders, saying, "Stuff happens." These jurors might be comfortable explaining the 2011 meltdown of three nuclear reactors in Fukushima following a 9.0 earthquake and tsunami as God's will. Stuff-happens jurors are also likely to believe that "everything happens for a reason."[22] Other comments we've heard over the years include "That's the way the cookie crumbles," "You reap what you sow," and "The chickens came home to roost."

The stuff-happens bias is one manifestation of the *just world* fallacy.[23] People like to believe that there is no such thing as undeserved suffering. They tend to attribute horrific events to a larger force for order, justice, or moral balance. Even unconsciously, they may rationalize that bad things don't happen to good people. Or they might conclude that, when bad things happen to good people, it is God's will or just a part of life and that human efforts to try to rectify the harm are misplaced.

---

[22] Paul Thagard, "Does Everything Happen for a Reason?" *Hot Thought* (blog), *Psychology Today*, February 11, 2010, https://www.psychologytoday.com/blog/hot-thought/201002/does-everything-happen-reason-0.

[23] Leo Montada and Melvin. J. Lerner, eds., *Responses to Victimizations and Belief in a Just World* (New York: Plenum Press, 1998), vii–viii; and Adrian Furnham, "Belief in a Just World: Research Progress over the Past Decade," *Personality and Individual Differences* 34 (April 2003): 795–817.

Cusimano once conducted a concept focus group in Las Vegas that he began, as he generally does, by providing very little information: "A wreck happened at the corner of Las Vegas Boulevard and Tropicana Avenue. What do you think happened?"[24]

His exchange with the focus group is a classic example of the stuff-happens bias at work:

> Focus Group: Somebody saw a truck coming and thought they'd get rich. Yeah, she was lucky; she might have been hurt worse if she hadn't been stopped at the intersection.
>
> Cusimano: Actually, she had the green light and the other driver ran the red light.
>
> Focus Group: She probably wasn't wearing a seat belt.
>
> Cusimano: Would that make a difference to you?
>
> Focus Group: Yes.
>
> Cusimano: She had on her seat belt.
>
> Focus Group: I bet she was driving some tiny little sports car.
>
> Cusimano: No, it was the largest Oldsmobile land barge they make.
>
> Focus Group: Hmm. They just don't make cars like they used to. Oh well, stuff happens.

This focus group was not ruling for the plaintiff, no matter the facts. Stuff-happens jurors believe that you just can't compensate

---

[24] We discuss concept focus groups in chapter 5, "Conducting Jury Research," page 89.

everybody who's hurt—injuries are part of life. The more uncertainty in the liability case or the more complex the fact pattern, the more likely it is that jurors will excuse the defendant's wrongdoing by concluding that stuff happens.

Psychologists Daniel Kahneman and Amos Tversky have published numerous articles about *heuristics*—mental shortcuts that allow us to think through a problem quickly and effortlessly, if not always accurately. Heuristics quicken our decision-making by letting us operate without deliberate thought about the next step. But because heuristics are shortcuts, they can lead us to make inaccurate judgments. Building on the work of Kahneman and Tversky, psychologists Susan Fiske and Shelley Taylor developed the *cognitive miser* theory to help further explain this behavior.[25]

Struggling to resolve a complex problem can lead to considerable anxiety. One way to escape that discomfort is to assume that no solution is required because all events are part of some overarching plan. Another way out is to throw up your hands in a stuff-happens gesture. The stuff-happens bias that Cusimano and Wenner identified in their research is really just a heuristic—a thinking substitute.

An indication that you're up against the stuff-happens bias is when your focus-group members pelt you with questions seeking more information. And at trial, you know you have a stuff-happens juror when someone demands a much higher level of proof or responds to closed-ended questions like this: "Well, I need to hear the whole case before I can answer that. I need more information." Panel members who are resistant during voir dire will likely be resistant stuff-happens jurors during closing argument.

It is unlikely you will change the minds of stuff-happens jurors during the course of a trial. Use voir dire or supplemental juror questionnaires to identify and strike them when you can. If you

---

[25] Susan T. Fiske and Shelley E. Taylor, *Social Cognition*, 2nd ed. (New York: McGraw-Hill, 1991).

find yourself with jurors who might be stuff-happens jurors, consider using *if only* or *counterfactual thinking*.

The idea is to look not only at the way things are, but also at how they could have been. Counterfactual thinking happens when we imagine how the damage could have been avoided. If we can conjure up numerous alternatives as to how the defendant could have acted differently to avert the damage, then the damage appears a greater tragedy and weakens the stuff-happens conclusion. The harder it is for jurors to think of a different result, the easier it is for them to conclude, "stuff happens." However, if you suggest several alternative decisions or actions that were available to the defendant and would have changed the outcome, this can lead jurors to think that "if only the defendant had . . ., then this wouldn't have happened." Getting jurors to think "if only" about the defendant's actions will invariably help your plaintiff's case. The more alternatives the defendant had to avoid the injury, the more likely the jury will find the defendant liable.

In considering the stuff-happens attitude, ask yourself these questions: Did the plaintiff contribute to his own harm or the tragic event and, if so, to what extent? Will the jury readily believe or imagine the result could have been easily avoided and, if so, by whom? Look for ways you can frame the facts to your advantage.

BIAS FIVE: BLAME THE PLAINTIFF

The fifth juror bias is the *blame-the-plaintiff* bias. In hundreds of focus groups, Cusimano and Wenner learned that jurors are frequently and unjustifiably likely to find fault with the plaintiff, even when contributory negligence is not an issue. Other researchers have also documented the existence of a blame-the-plaintiff bias. In one survey, 80 percent of people complained that plaintiffs are too quick to sue rather than settle disputes.[26] In another study, researchers found a blame-the-victim phenomenon in the trial context.[27] There are ample studies available on victim blaming.

One study by Neal Feigenson, Jaihyun Park, and Peter Salovey clearly illustrates the blame-the-plaintiff bias. Participants determined liability and damages based on the following general facts:

> Hocon Gas, the defendant, provided propane fuel to Mr. and Mrs. Roe's residence. There was a thirty-year-old valve that controlled the flow of propane from the tank (owned by Hocon) to the Roes' appliances in the house. Hocon's insurance company had asked Hocon to replace all valves that were over fifteen years old. Unfortunately, the Roes' valve had not been replaced.
>
> One day, Mr. Roe smelled gas and heard a hissing from the kitchen. A telephone repairman was working outside on the property, so Mr. Roe asked him if he would help investigate. When they entered the kitchen, the noise was so loud the repairman yelled, "Let's get the hell out of here!"
>
> The house exploded as they ran from it. The repairman was not injured, but Mr. Roe was and he died seven days later. Thankfully, Mr. Roe was the only one home though Mrs. Roe had just had a baby five months previously.[28]

---

[26] Valerie P. Hans, "The Contested Role of the Civil Jury in Business Litigation," *Judicature* 79, no. 5 (1996): 242, 244.

[27] Kelly G. Shaver, "Defensive Attribution: Effects of Severity and Relevance on the Responsibility Assigned for an Accident," *Journal of Personality and Social Psychology* 14 (February 1970): 101.

[28] Neal Feigenson, Jaihyun Park, and Peter Salovey, "Effect of Blameworthiness and Outcome Severity on Attributions of Responsibility and Damage Awards in Comparative Negligence Cases," *Law and Human Behavior* 21, no. 6 (1997).

When they analyzed the results of their experiment, the researchers discovered that jurors decided the case based on legally irrelevant matters that were harmful to the plaintiffs' case. At times, study subjects made up evidence—the plaintiff caused the leak or the plaintiff was responsible for the faulty valve—even though the facts did not permit such inferences. Psychologists have long known that people fill in the gaps of a story to fit their own view of the facts.[29]

In the 1960s, British psychologist Peter Wason published the results of a number of studies exploring what Wason termed the *confirmation bias*, the tendency of people to interpret information in a way that confirms their preexisting beliefs.[30] Other researchers refer to the phenomenon as the *myside bias*, since people evaluate and generate evidence in a way that supports their side and refutes or ignores the opposing side.[31] The science confirms what Wenner and Cusimano observed: people will repeatedly invent facts that are detrimental to the plaintiff's case.

What accounts for this laser-like focus on plaintiffs' conduct to explain the cause of their injuries? Several different principles are at play, including: *defensive attribution*, *ideal self*, and the *fundamental attribution error*.

---

[29] Scott Plous, *The Psychology of Judgment and Decision Making* (Columbus: McGraw-Hill, 1993).

[30] Peter C. Wason, "On the Failure to Eliminate Hypotheses in a Conceptual Task," *Quarterly Journal of Experimental Psychology* 12 (July 1960): 129–140.

[31] Keith E. Stanovich, Richard. F. West, and Maggie E. Toplak, "Myside Bias, Rational Thinking, and Intelligence," *Current Directions in Psychological Science* 22, no. 4 (August 5, 2013): 259–264.

Defensive Attribution

When someone is injured, people (this proclivity is not limited to jurors) are inclined to blame the person who was hurt.[32] This act of defensive attribution helps us to dodge the fear that the same thing could happen to us through no fault of our own. Some research shows that the more alike a person may be to someone who was harmed or involved in a tragic event, the more likely that person is to blame the injured party. The degree of the similarity changes the attribution of blame placed on the person harmed.

As discussed before, people feel a need to believe in a just world—a place where bad things do not happen to good people. They want a predictable world over which they have some measure of control through their actions. When a good person suffers undeservedly, their image of a just world is at risk of disappearing. Rather than acknowledge that injustice, people resort to condemning the injured plaintiff. The worse the plaintiff's injuries, the greater the likelihood that people will raise the shield of defensive attribution.[33] Cusimano's stuff-happens focus-group respondents were likely motivated to create repeated stumbling blocks to the plaintiff's recovery because accepting the idea that anyone could be injured or killed on a sunny day in Las Vegas when another driver runs a red light frightened them. Many of these anti-plaintiff attitudes, including defensive attribution, make people blame the plaintiff.

Defensive attribution can lead to harsh results. In one of the focus groups Cusimano and Wenner conducted for a breast cancer case during their ATLA research, a male participant asked,

---

[32] Indeed, trial lawyers are also guilty of the defensive-attribution bias, as we discuss in chapter 5, page 101.

[33] Melvin J. Lerner and Julie H. Goldberg, "When Do Decent People Blame Victims?: The Differing Effects of the Explicit/Rational and Implicit/Experiental Cognitive Systems," in *Dual-Process Theories in Social Psychology*, eds. Shelly Chaiken and Yaacov Trope (New York: Guilford Press, 1999), 627–640.

"This woman had three children and a husband. Shouldn't they at least receive something to cover the burial expense?"

A forty-year-old woman in the group retorted, "She should have thought about those children when she chose not to see another doctor. Besides, everybody dies and everybody has funeral expenses." Wenner had an extremely difficult time processing this response on a moral level. The woman's ostensible cruelty, in fact, is what prompted Wenner to seek out psychologist Lee Ross at Stanford. Defensive attribution has the power to destroy all empathy in an otherwise decent human being.

Ideal Self

When jurors judge a plaintiff's behavior (or anyone's behavior), they reflexively compare the plaintiff's conduct to what they would have done in the same circumstance. The hitch is that jurors make that assessment based on what their best or ideal self would have done—not their real, flawed self. For example, when someone else's child runs unsupervised through a restaurant and bumps into your chair, sending a twelve-dollar glass of Malbec onto the Italian silk tie your daughter gave you for your birthday, it's easy to forget the time your five-year-old sprayed apple juice through a straw at an elderly couple.

Jurors generally do not approach their task with the self-awareness required to ask, "Have I ever acted like that?" Instead they muse, "How would I act if confronted with that situation?" By judging the plaintiff's conduct against the hypothetical actions of their ideal self, jurors fail to acknowledge the human frailty to which everyone is prone. As a result, they tend to blame the plaintiff.

Countering the defensive-attribution and ideal-self biases requires thought and planning. One way to do this is to create a way for jurors to place themselves in a similar situation to the plaintiff in the abstract, before they are given the facts of the case. For example, you can use voir dire to educate the jury on a normal reaction to a situation. In a slip and fall case, you can help jurors understand that the plaintiff's response was normal by asking them to think of a time when they may have slipped or missed a chair they planned to sit in and immediately tried to recover without acknowledging the mishap. You can ask if they were embarrassed and got up quickly, hoping others didn't see what happened. When jurors realize the plaintiff's conduct was normal, it may help them understand why someone didn't report a fall immediately or seek immediate medical help.

Fundamental Attribution Error

The fundamental attribution error, a term coined by psychologist Lee Ross, leads people to attribute a person's choices and conduct to some personal shortcoming or character flaw rather than the situation in which he finds himself.[34] As psychologists describe the bias, the person is more "salient" in the jurors' minds than the situation. This leads people to blame the plaintiff.

For instance, people may assume that a plaintiff who tripped in a department store was injured because he was careless and inattentive. Our natural focus is on the person and not on the situation—the department store's oversized color poster advertising a semi-annual underwear sale was placed above a water spill on the white marble floor caused by a leaking drinking fountain. The fundamental attribution error causes jurors to focus on the plaintiff's inattention and not the distracting store displays and wet floor that caused him to trip. The phenomenon is called the fundamental attribution error because of its pervasiveness and because we are unaware of its effect on our judgment.

---

[34] *See* Lee Ross, "The Intuitive Psychologist and His Shortcomings: Distortions in the Attribution Process," in *Advances in Experimental Psychology,* ed. Leonard Berkowitz (Academic Press, 1977), 10: 173–220; and Lee Ross and Richard E. Nisbett, *The Person and the Situation: Perspectives of Social Psychology* (McGraw-Hill, 1991).

The way to combat the fundamental attribution error is to build a case that explains the plaintiff's conduct in terms of his situation, helplessly distracted by the department store's deliberately provocative displays (situation more salient than individual). The defendant merchant, on the other hand, was more focused on profiting from lingerie sales than keeping the store's flooring safe for its unsuspecting patrons (individual more salient than situation).

In any lawsuit, all three of these principles—defensive attribution, ideal self, and fundamental attribution error—may combine to create the blame-the-plaintiff bias. Unfortunately, the principles are far more likely to damage the plaintiff's case than the defendant's. The antidote for the blame-the-plaintiff bias, as we will discuss,[35] is to reframe your case by developing facts and crafting a trial story that removes focus from the plaintiff's conduct and directs attention toward the defendant's.

Suspicion, victimization, personal responsibility, stuff happens, and blame the plaintiff are the five biases, or attitudes, that Cusimano and Wenner identified twenty years ago in their original research for the Jury Bias Model. In this age of continuing assault on plaintiffs and the civil jury trial, it is not possible to build an effective case without identifying, understanding, and combatting these biases.

We should recognize that these attitudes that often operate as anti-plaintiff are not necessarily distinct and independent. They interact and are entwined. It is possible to see all five in a fact pattern or—more likely—to see two or three. Try to analyze and recognize them in your case so you can counter their influence if they work against you and enhance their effect if they work for you. Using the Jury Bias Model's Ten Commandments, as explained in the next chapter, will help you reach the result you seek.

---

[35] *See* discussion on page 56.

WHAT WE HAVE LEARNED

Cusimano and Wenner based the Jury Bias Model on thousands of hours spent studying the academic literature and consulting with some of the nation's leading scholars. In addition, the pair conducted hundreds of focus groups in which they tried and tested the application of well-documented psychological principles to the arena of plaintiffs' tort litigation.

As you begin preparation in any case, be mindful of the five jury biases described in the model:

1. Suspicion
2. Victimization
3. Personal Responsibility
4. Stuff Happens
5. Blame the Plaintiff

The next chapter will discuss the Ten Commandments of the Jury Bias Model—counteractive measures designed specifically to combat the five jury biases and strengthen your presentation.

2

THE JURY BIAS MODEL
PART TWO
The Ten Commandments

The Jury Bias Model does more than outline a problem. Its Ten Commandments provide a strategy for overcoming the effects of the five juror biases while you build an effective case for your clients. Many of these commandments are based on heuristics that we all use to simplify our own decision-making process. Incorporate these commandments into your case to combat jury bias.

1. COMPOSE A TRIAL STORY

Research confirms what many trial lawyers already know: people learn and remember by listening to stories.[1] Indeed, we

---

[1] Roger C. Schank and Robert P. Abelson, "Knowledge and Memory: The Real Story," in *Knowledge and Memory: The Real Story* ed. Robert S. Wyer

devote an entire chapter in this book to our ideas on how to develop an effective trial story.[2] Focus jurors' attention on how the defendant's conduct harmed the plaintiff, why the defendant is responsible, and why it's fair and necessary to compensate the plaintiff. Include decisions the defendant made over a long period of time. A story about a single day in the plaintiff's life leads the jury to focus on the plaintiff, while a story about a premeditated or ignored scheme and a long course of inaction draws jurors' attention to the defendant's conduct. Make your story simple and include a moral. Rely on the remaining nine commandments to make that story memorable and to emphasize the parts your jurors already believed in when they arrived on day one at the courthouse.

2. ELICIT CONFIRMATION

As we just discussed in reference to the blame-the-plaintiff bias, the confirmation bias is the tendency of people to listen for and remember information that confirms what they already believe.[3] In their focus-group research, Cusimano and Wenner consistently recorded participants' willingness to accept, without analysis, facts that supported their beliefs. But when the facts challenged participants' preconceived ideas, they fought vehemently rather than accept the evidence as true. This is why it's important to

---

(Hillsdale, N.J: Lawrence Erlbaum Associates, 1995). Available at http://cog-prints.org/636/1/KnowledgeMemory_SchankAbelson_d.html.

[2] *See* chapter 7, "Developing the Trial Story," page 127.

[3] *See generally* Raymond S. Nickerson, "Confirmation Bias: A Ubiquitous Phenomenon in Many Guises," *Review of General Psychology* 2, no. 2 (June 1998): 175–220; and Patricia G. Devine, Edward R. Hirt, and Elizabeth M. Gehrke, "Diagnostic and Confirmation Strategies in Trait Hypothesis Testing," *Journal of Personality and Social Psychology* 58, no. 6 (1990): 952–963.

develop a trial story that confirms, rather than conflicts with, what jurors already believe. Work with the confirmation bias; it is much easier to incorporate a juror's belief than to change it.

Understanding confirmation bias requires an exploration of *schemas*.[4] A schema is a cognitive file cabinet for organizing facts, beliefs, and ideas. A prototype is a *role schema* that helps us predict how a person will behave in a given situation. A script is an *event schema* that allows us to envision how a certain event should unfold. When we encounter a new experience, a schema gives us a cognitive framework for making sense of the new information.

Schemas influence our perceptions. If a person does not behave as our role schema tells us he should, we begin to wonder what's wrong with him. If an event does not take place as we predicted, we begin searching for the cause of our unmet expectations. Use focus groups early to learn the likely schemas that jurors will use to interpret the evidence in your case. What beliefs, theories, and expectations emerge toward the parties, causation, and damages? Once you identify important schemas, investigate the facts to develop a trial story that's consistent with jurors' likely beliefs and expectations. If the plaintiff's conduct is consistent with jurors' schemas, they are much more likely to believe in the plaintiff's case.

Jurors are not the only people with schemas in their heads. Defense lawyers, insurance adjusters, and judges will all rely on schemas to evaluate your lawsuit. In a well-known experiment by Stanford psychologist David L. Rosenhan, eight subjects (three of whom were psychologists) were presented to a psychiatric hospital.[5] Upon arrival, all of the pseudo-patients complained to the unsuspecting hospital staff that they were

---

[4] First used in philosophy, *schemas* were described by Jean Piaget in the 1920s. It is a concept that results in taking shortcuts in organizing and understanding information. It is a heuristic that people use to simplify facts and data.

[5] David L. Rosenhan, "On Being Sane in Insane Places," *Science* 179, no. 4070 (January 1973): 250–258.

hearing voices. None of the pseudo-patients had ever been diagnosed with any psychological problem.

The hospital staff admitted all but one of the pseudo-patients with a diagnosis of schizophrenia. Upon admission, the symptoms ceased. Still, the hospital staff instructed that the pseudo-patients could not be released until they convinced the staff of their sanity. The schemas that highly trained hospital staff used in diagnosing psychiatric patients biased their perception of the perfectly sane pseudo-patients. When the pseudo-patients took notes during their stay, for example, the staff attributed the activity to the compulsive writing behavior associated with schizophrenia. Ultimately, the hospital released the pseudo-patients—but it was with a diagnosis of schizophrenia in remission. Even psychiatrists fall prey to the confirmation bias.

At trial, the confirmation bias leads jurors to have better recall of evidence that confirms their schemas.[6] When people are bombarded with information for days at a time, they lose their ability to recall information that's incongruent with their beliefs—perhaps because they lack sufficient cognitive reserves to reconcile the inconsistencies.[7] As a result, your trial story will be more memorable when it portrays the plaintiff in a role that fits with jurors' schemas.

The other type of evidence that jurors are likely to remember is something that is sharply at odds with their schemas. Make the defendant's misconduct memorable by vividly describing it in terms that highlight his divergence from jurors' schemas.

---

[6] *See* Richard E. Nisbett and Lee Ross, *Human Inference: Strategies and Shortcomings of Social Judgment* (Prentice Hall, 1980); and Lee Ross et al., "Perseverance in Self-Perception and Social Perception: Biased Attributional Processing in the Debriefing Paradigm," *Journal of Personality and Social Psychology* 32, no. 880 (1975); and Amos Tversky and Daniel Kahneman, "Judgment Under Uncertainty: Heuristics and Biases," *Science* 185, no. 1124 (1974).

[7] *See generally* Thomas K. Srull et al., "Associative Storage and Retrieval Processes in Person Memory," *Journal of Experimental Psychology: Learning, Memory and Cognition* 11, no. 316 (1985).

Schemas are particularly important during jury selection. For instance, a juror who frequently visits the emergency room with her sick child will have a well-developed schema about the respective roles of an emergency room doctor and a specialist. In a medical negligence case, she will likely assign less blame to an emergency room doctor than to a specialist because, in her experience, the specialist is the one with superior knowledge and responsibility for a patient's diagnosis and care. This juror's particular schema will exert a powerful bias on her view of the evidence. You need to know that during voir dire.

Utilizing schemas that resonate with your jurors also allows you to establish a rapport with them. *Utilization* is a tool long used in psychotherapy to foster trust and cooperation in which the therapist accepts and utilizes the patient's beliefs and convictions during treatment. At trial, listen for, accept, and then utilize the information that panel members disclose about their values and interests. In one of our cases, for example, a juror volunteered that he had "three children living." The addition of the word "living" told us that the juror had experienced the death of a child. That would be important to any parent. We accepted the communication and then utilized it later by incorporating the fact into our trial story. Jurors saw that we were listening and that we understood and cared about what was important to them. The jurors became active participants in the trial with us. Being sensitive to the jurors' important schemas made this dialog possible.

Never underestimate the extent to which people's prior experiences influence their perception of the evidence. Make the confirmation bias work for you by using focus groups to identify the schemas that persuasively fit your case. Then develop a trial story that emphasizes those schemas. In the final analysis, a person's core belief will prevail over any evidence that challenges that belief.[8]

---

[8] For more on juror beliefs, *see* chapter 9, "Understanding and Applying Beliefs," page 169.

3. REMEMBER THAT BELIEFS PERSEVERE

Belief perseverance leads people to cling to a story once they've adopted it as their own, even in the face of later conflicting or discrediting evidence.[9] In their research, Wenner and Cusimano repeatedly witnessed focus-group respondents maintain their initial version of events despite later learning that their position had no evidentiary support. The way to make this heuristic work for you is to tell the story of the defendant's egregious conduct as early as possible in a way that's consistent with the jurors' pretrial beliefs so they will adopt this version as their own.[10] Once they are invested, jurors tend to discount, or underweight, subsequent conflicting evidence—no matter how compelling.

In a dramatic example of belief perseverance at work, psychologists conducted an experiment in which they instructed study participants to read twenty-five pairs of suicide notes and decide which of each pair was genuine.[11] As the subjects read the notes, other study participants observed. When the subjects finished with the notes, researchers told half of them that they had been very successful in their determination and the other half that they had performed poorly. After giving the subjects

---

[9] *See* Nisbett and Ross, *supra* note 19, at 167; *see also*, C.A. Anderson, "Belief Perseverance" in *Encyclopedia of Social Psychology*, eds. Roy. F. Baumeister and Kathleen D. Vohs (Los Angeles: SAGE Publications, 2007): 109–110; and Deanna Khun and Joseph Lao, "Effects of Evidence on Attitudes: Is Polarization the Norm?" *Psychological Science* 7, no. 2 (March 1996): 115–120.

[10] Of course, you have discovered their beliefs and attitudes from your jury research.

[11] D. M. Wegner, G. Coulton, and R. Wenzlaff, "The Transparency of Denial: Briefing in the Debriefing Paradigm," *Journal of Personality and Social Psychology* 49, no. 2 (1985): 382–391.

this initial feedback, the researchers then informed them that the feedback had been entirely made up and did not reflect their actual performance. Next, researchers asked the subjects and observers how well the subjects would perform in a second round of determining the authenticity of a different group of suicide notes. Everyone—the subjects who read the notes and those who merely observed the process—predicted that those who had been "successful" on the first round would perform better than the other group. The subjects persevered in their beliefs, even after being told that those beliefs were based on a sham.

This is also true for focus groups. Participants do not continually update their understanding of the trial story as new evidence is introduced. Instead, new evidence that is consistent with the respondents' adopted trial story tends to bolster it. Inconsistent evidence is more likely to receive critical scrutiny. Jurors construct a story that confirms their prior beliefs (confirmation bias), and that story perseveres even in the wake of inconsistent evidence (belief perseverance).

One example of this is from a case where the plaintiff ran head-on into a guardrail. Unfortunately, the guardrail had been installed backward. Instead of collapsing as designed, it speared the vehicle and its occupants. We asked focus-group respondents what they thought would happen if a car ran head-on into a guardrail. Some thought it would be designed to collapse, some thought it would spear the vehicle, and some weren't sure.

We then showed them video of the guardrail design being tested, where test vehicles run into the guardrail and it collapses—as designed. Those who thought it would collapse thought the video showed it collapsing. Those who thought it would spear a vehicle thought the video showed the guardrail spearing the test vehicles. Those who weren't sure, weren't sure what they saw. They all saw the exact same footage at the exact same time, yet reached different conclusions about what happened based on their prior beliefs.

Use belief perseverance to your advantage by presenting your strongest evidence first. Evidence that is presented early and then frequently reinforced remains vivid for jurors who are more apt to use it for processing subsequent evidence. In effect, you prime your jurors to interpret evidence throughout the trial in a way that confirms what they already believe and that allows them to persevere in those beliefs. Psychologists have long understood that priming influences a person's judgment. The eminent social psychologist Solomon Asch demonstrated the point in a 1946 experiment in which researchers asked subjects to evaluate an individual based on the following two descriptions:

1. Steve is intelligent, industrious, impulsive, critical, stubborn, and envious.
2. Steve is envious, stubborn, critical, impulsive, industrious, and intelligent.

The statements contain exactly the same words, but in reverse order. What Asch found was that study subjects described the "intelligent" Steve as a capable person whose faults did not outweigh his merits. But subjects viewed the "envious" Steve as a problem. In addition, when subjects were primed to see Steve in a positive light, they interpreted ambiguous words such as "impulsive" and "critical" as favorable, as opposed to negative, traits.[12]

Priming and belief perseverance work together to confirm and perpetuate jurors' initial view of the defendant's conduct in your case. Your trial story of the defendant's misconduct must be seeded during voir dire, told in opening statement, retold with the evidence, and reinforced during closing argument. That's how to create the most powerful influence over the jurors' decision-making process.

---

[12] Solomon E. Asch, "Forming Impressions of Personality," *The Journal of Abnormal and Social Psychology* 41 (July 1946): 258–290.

4. Sequence the Available Evidence

People make decisions based on information that is readily available in their memory. That's the *availability bias*.[13] The way to use this knowledge to your advantage at trial is to ensure that jurors receive a wealth of information about the defendant's wrongdoing. If you focus your trial story on the defendant's conduct, then jurors will focus on the defendant's conduct when they deliberate. They will decide your case based on the evidence that is most available in their minds.

Everyone is subject to the availability bias. People's perceptions are influenced by the information that is readily available to them. For example, people generally assume that gun deaths by murder are more common than by suicide—though the opposite is true, and by a wide margin.[14] This is a common assumption because school shootings, and other killings involving guns, are widely and sensationally reported. Not so for suicides. Instances of gun violence involving murder are more readily available in our memories, so we wrongly assume that gun deaths by murder are more common.

Psychologists have conducted exhaustive research on the effects of the availability bias on judgment. In one experiment,

---

[13] *See generally* Thomas Gilovich, Dale Griffin, and Daniel Kahneman, eds., *Heuristics and Biases: The Psychology of Intuitive Judgment* (Cambridge: Cambridge University Press, 2002); and Amos Tversky and Daniel Kahneman, "Availability: A Heuristic for Judging Frequency and Probability," *Cognitive Psychology* 5, no. 2 (1973): 207–232, doi:10.1016/0010-0285(73)90033-9.

[14] Margot Sanger-Katz, "Gun Deaths Are Mostly Suicides," *New York Times*, October 8, 2015, http://www.nytimes.com/2015/10/09/upshot/gun-deaths-are-mostly-suicides.html.

subjects were given a description of Mr. Jones, a forty-seven-year-old father of three whose wife had been sick for several months.

One day, Mr. Jones left the bank where he worked at his regular time, though he had often been leaving early to take care of chores his wife asked him to do. He didn't go home along his regular route as it was a clear day and he wanted to drive along the shore to enjoy the view.

As he was approaching a major intersection, the light turned amber. A witness noticed that he braked hard to stop at the crossing, although he easily could have gone through. His family recognized this as a typical habit when he was driving. As he began to cross after the light turned back to green, a truck raced through the intersection at top speed and hit Mr. Jones's car from the left, killing him on impact. The truck was driven by a teenage boy who was under the influence of drugs. When hearing about what happened in the days following, his family and friends often thought and said, "If only . . .".

The psychologists conducting the study then asked those who read this description to complete the last sentence. They asked, "How did they continue the thought? Please write one or more likely completions."[15]

After reading the story, only 21 percent of the subjects finished the sentence by eliminating the drug-crazed truck driver from the scene. Instead, the subjects directed their focus to Mr. Jones's conduct, with a majority of subjects completing the thought like this: "If only Mr. Jones had taken another route."[16]

This experiment powerfully illustrates how the availability bias works. The focus of the story was on Mr. Jones and the route he took home on a beautiful sunny day. The subjects who

---

[15] *See generally* Daniel Kahneman and Amos Tversky, "The Simulation Heuristic," in *Judgment Under Uncertainty: Heuristics and Biases* eds. Daniel Kahneman, Paul Slovic, and Amos Tversky (Cambridge University Press, 1982): 201–208.

[16] *Id.*

analyzed the incident drew from the information available to them to focus their attention on Mr. Jones, rather than the driver who killed him.

For trial lawyers, the message is clear. Focus your trial story on what's important to your case—the defendant's misconduct—and eliminate extraneous information that could distract jurors' attention from that focus.

Cusimano had a case in the Smoky Mountains where a chalet slid down a mountain as a result of a propane leak and explosion that occurred under the occupied part of the structure. When he told the story starting with the couple who rented the chalet, what they were doing, and that they were the first renters after construction, the focus-group participants imagined actions the couple did took cause the explosion or hypothesized that since it was new, settling could have occurred to cause the leak—some even hypothesized that a tremor in North Carolina in the same mountain strata could have caused the leak.

When Cusimano started the story with the builder, the builder's efforts to cut costs, and how the builder's own crew installed the propane fireplace—rather than the company that sold the fireplace—Cusimano heard no more about settling, tremors, or fault of the couple who rented the chalet.

5. HEED THE NORM

Jurors reason backward from an outcome and look for unusual elements in the story leading up to it. They ask themselves, "If the unusual piece is eliminated, does the result change?" Under the norm bias, the further from the norm, or more unusual, the defendant's conduct is, the more likely it is that jurors will blame him.[17] To use the norm bias to your advantage, include unusual facts about the defendant and his conduct in your trial story. When the defendant's conduct appears entirely ordinary, jurors are not inclined to impose liability. But when the defendant's conduct departs from the norm, jurors are more likely to find causation. In many cases, you can rely on governmental regulations, industry standards, or other rules to establish the norm and then show how the defendant departed from it.

One example of using regulations to establish a norm comes from a case where a commercial truck driver consistently complained about exhaust in the cab of the truck she was driving. The maintenance company deferred upkeep on it, and the truck driver passed out one day from carbon monoxide poisoning, resulting in a permanent brain injury. Federal rules require that no truck be on the road if there are issues of exhaust leaking into the cab. If the maintenance company hadn't deviated from the norm by ignoring federal regulations, the driver wouldn't have been injured.

If you tell this story from the experience of the driver, with her complaining about the smell of exhaust but driving anyway until one day she passes out, focus-group respondents want to blame the driver for getting into the cab of the truck despite smelling exhaust fumes. Respondents consider the driver's behavior a deviation from the norm. But when told from the perspective of the maintenance company, the norm shifts and the defendants are the ones who are deviating from the norm and who, therefore, are liable.

---

[17] *See generally* M. Sherif, *The Psychology of Social Norms* (New York: Harper, 1936); M. K. Lapinski and R. N. Rimal, "An Explication of Social Norms," *Communication Theory* 15, no. 2 (2005): 127–147; Guillermina Jasso, "Rule Finding About Rule Making: Comparison Processes and the Making of Rules," in *Social Norms*, eds. Michael Hechter and Karl-Dieter Opp (Russell Sage Foundation, 2001): 348–393, http://www.jstor.org/stable/10.7758/9781610442800.

6. REVERSE THE FUNDAMENTAL ATTRIBUTION ERROR

We have already explained how the fundamental attribution error contributes to the blame-the-plaintiff bias.[18] The fundamental attribution error describes the tendency of people to attribute a person's choices and conduct to a personal shortcoming rather than to the situation in which she finds herself.[19]

As a result, your trial story must show that the plaintiff behaved as she did because of external circumstances beyond her control, not because of internal shortcomings. Further, the defendant's conduct was not based on circumstances, but on a *character stain*—a character flaw or hidden, selfish motive.

For example, we had a case where a college student was hit by a car when crossing a busy street. Focus-group respondents assumed that she was rushing across the street and being a careless, crazy kid. That changed when we showed them that the timing of the light at the intersection made it so that no one could get across by walking if they left at the time the walk signal turned green. The light would change and trap anyone in the intersection if they were not rushing or running. The defendant was the government entity that set the light this way, and we focused on their failure to correct it because it would require extra cost. The light was at the entrance to a college campus where the defendant knew a lot of college students crossed back and forth.

---

[18] *See* chapter 1, "The Jury Bias Model Part One," page 37.

[19] *See generally* Edward E. Jones and Victor A. Harris, "The Attribution of Attitudes," *Journal of Experimental Social Psychology* 3, no. 1 (1967): 1–24, https://doi.org/10.1016/0022-1031(67)90034-0; http://lee.ross.socialpsychology.org; and Lee Ross and Richard E. Nisbett, *The Person and the Situation: Perspectives of Social Psychology* (London: Pinter & Martin Ltd., 2011).

In another example, a lawyer we know worked on a case where a nighttime security guard was injured on his break when the ladder-backed wood chair he was sitting on collapsed. The manufacturer was sued. The focus group assumed the guard fell asleep while he was leaning the chair backward against a wall, and that is when the chair broke. They blamed the plaintiff. When they learned the security guard found and turned in a diamond bracelet the month before, they found for the plaintiff. Believing he was of outstanding character made a difference in the outcome.

7. Plan for the Hindsight Bias

Similar to Monday-morning quarterbacking, the hindsight bias is the tendency to believe after the fact that an event was predictable.[20] The hindsight bias is often useful in a trial story to emphasize what the defendant should have known, though the bias may also be effective in a defendant's trial story where the plaintiff has been comparatively or contributory negligent.

Think of any case where maintenance or medical care was delayed or denied, or a case where a driver is texting or talking on the phone. The examples used earlier in this chapter all lend themselves to a trial story that takes advantage of the hindsight bias. What did the municipality expect would happen when setting the timing on a stoplight so pedestrians could not get across the street in time without running? Or what did the trucking company and its maintenance subcontractor think would happen when delaying maintenance on an exhaust leak? Anytime

---

[20] *See generally* B. Fischhoff and R. Beyth, "'I Knew It Would Happen': Remembered Probabilities of Once-Future Things," *Organizational Behavior and Human Performance*, 13 (1975), 1–16; B. Fischhoff, "Hindsight ≠ Foresight: The Effect of Outcome Knowledge on Judgment under Uncertainty," *Quality and Safety in Health Care* 12 (2003): 304–312.

you can pose the rhetorical question "What did they expect would happen if . . . ?" you have a case where the hindsight bias can come into play.

8. CREATE EMPATHY

Empathy is the capacity for sharing the feelings and experiences of someone else.[21] It has been described as a cognitive bias. Often empathy engenders compassion, the desire to mitigate injury or harm and even do something about it. When jurors lack empathy for the plaintiff, they tend to show partiality for the defendant. Accordingly, use your trial story to create empathy for the plaintiff by emphasizing facts that show him to be credible, hardworking, optimistic, and a valued member of the community. This is a good tool for combating defensive attribution.

9. DROP THE ANCHOR

An anchor is a fact we use as a reference point, often in regard to a sum of money. The initial sum becomes an anchor. People are likely to decide on a fair price for something by starting with the anchor and adjusting up or down from there. At trial, jurors will under- or overadjust from a suggested anchor in reaching a decision on damages, depending on their perception of the reasonableness of the anchor. A higher anchor tends to yield higher

---

[21] *See generally* S. D. Hodges and K. J. K. Klein, "Regulating the Costs of Empathy: The Price of Being Human," *Journal of Socio-Economics* (2001); and C. D. Batson, "These Things Called Empathy: Eight Related but Distinct Phenomena," *The Social Neuroscience of Empathy*, eds. J. Decety and W. Ickes (Cambridge, MA: MIT Press, 2009), 3–15.

awards because of a bias toward the anchor.[22] For example, researchers have found that in salary negotiations, when the initial salary number is set arbitrarily high, the ultimate negotiated salary is more likely to be higher as well.[23]

Given this knowledge, anchoring can be particularly useful in making a specific damages request part of your trial story—if done properly and ethically, and if allowed in the venue.

10. BUILD THE FRAME

Use reframing to structure the facts so jurors can see that the trial story is consistent with their own existing beliefs. Different presentations of the same issues or facts influence choices and judgments.[24]

As we discussed concerning the first three of the five anti-plaintiff biases—suspicion, victimization, and blame the plaintiff—reframe your case to blunt the impact of these biases. One of the most effective tools available to you is *loss framing*. Loss framing directs jurors' attention away from concerns that they themselves will be victimized by a plaintiff's verdict by

---

[22] *See generally* Amos Tversky and Daniel Kahneman, "Judgment under Uncertainty: Heuristics and Biases," *Science* 185, no. 4157 (1974), 1124–1131, doi:10.1126/science.185.4157.1124. PMID 1783547.

[23] T. J. Thorsteinson, "Initiating Salary Discussions with an Extreme Request: Anchoring Effects on Initial Salary Offers," *Journal of Applied Social Psychology* 41 (2011): 1774–1792, doi: 10.1111/j.1559-1816.2011.00779.x.

[24] *See generally* Amos Tversky and Daniel Kahneman, "The Framing of Decisions and the Psychology of Choice," *Science* 211, no. 4481 (1981): 453–458, doi:10.1126/science.7455683. PMID 7455683; and A. K. Thomas and P. R. Millar, "Reducing the Framing Effect in Older and Younger Adults by Encouraging Analytic Processing," *The Journals of Gerontology Series B: Psychological Sciences and Social Sciences* 67B, no. 2 (2011): 139, doi:10.1093/geronb/gbr076.

illustrating that, instead, the plaintiff's case will actually benefit the jurors by keeping their community safe.[25]

Tread carefully, however. It is intuitive to assume that jurors would welcome the opportunity to make their communities safer by raising the bar for all manufacturers, health-care professionals, or premises owners, for example. By finding for the plaintiff, jurors should be reassured that they stand to gain a safer world. This assumption, however, is dead wrong.

Psychologists Kahneman and Tversky, and their now quite well-known research on prospect theory and loss aversion,[26] demonstrate that people are more motivated by the prospect of losing something they already own than the hope of gaining something they do not possess. Your goal, then, is to frame a decision for the plaintiff as a protection of the status quo—the safe community in which the jurors already live. Ruling for the defendant would amount to the affirmation of conduct that doesn't live up to existing standards. A defense verdict would lead to the loss of the jurors' safe world.

To use loss framing effectively, you must first understand two related psychological principles: loss aversion and the status quo bias.

LOSS AVERSION

People would rather avoid a loss than achieve a gain. In fact, Tversky and Kahneman's research demonstrates that we feel the pain of loss more acutely than the pleasure of gain, making us

---

[25] For further discussion of loss framing in other contexts, *see* chapter 7, "Developing the Trial Story," page 127.

[26] Psychologists Daniel Kahneman and Amos Tversky introduced prospect theory and loss aversion in 1979. In 2002, after Tversky's death, Kahneman was awarded the Nobel Prize in economics for the theories.

two times more motivated to avoid a loss than to acquire a gain.[27] As marketers know, people would rather avoid a 10 percent surcharge than receive a 10 percent discount, even though there is no financial distinction between the two.

In one study, researchers offered subjects $50 and asked them to choose between keeping $30 or gambling $50 with a fifty-fifty chance of keeping (or losing) the full amount. Most subjects chose the loss-averse option and decided not to gamble. Then researchers reframed the exact same choice. After offering them $50, they asked subjects to decide between losing $20 or gambling $50 with a fifty-fifty chance of winning or losing the entire $50. The substantial majority (61.6 percent) chose to gamble rather than lose $20.[28] Loss aversion is not rational, but it is powerfully real.

STATUS QUO BIAS

An emotional bias that is related to loss aversion, and equally important for trial lawyers to understand, is the status quo bias. Rather than make a change that might be perceived as a loss, people have an emotional bias toward the status quo; we tend to leave things as they are. The status quo bias causes people to use the present state as a baseline, from which they intuitively perceive any change as a possible loss.[29] The alternative to loss, real or imagined, is maintaining the status quo—doing nothing.

---

[27] Daniel Kahneman and Amos Tversky, "Choices, Values, and Frames," *American Psychologist* 39, no. 4 (1984): 341–350.

[28] Benedetto De Martino, Dharshan Kumaran, Ben Seymour, and Raymond J. Dolan, "Frames, Biases, and Rational Decision-Making in the Human Brain," *Science* 313, no. 5787 (August 2006): 684–687.

[29] William Samuelson and Richard Zeckhauser, "Status Quo Bias in Decision Making," *Journal of Risk and Uncertainty* 1 (1988): 7–59.

The status quo bias works hand in glove with rules on burden of proof to make the trial lawyer's job particularly challenging. When jurors leave things in a lawsuit where they find them, the only option is a defense verdict—the status quo. In post-trial interviews, we often learn that jurors didn't necessarily side with the defense; they just didn't feel motivated to upset the status quo. In their view, they simply left both sides as they had been. This decision is not entirely because the jurors were inclined to follow the trial court's instruction on the plaintiff's burden of proof. Jurors, like everyone else, have a psychological predisposition to maintain the status quo.

Loss framing takes the psychological principles of loss aversion and the status quo bias and flips them around to the plaintiff's advantage.

Tort reformers have taught suspicious jurors that they and their families will be victimized by jackpot-justice lawsuits that threaten their choice of health care, the price of their consumer goods, and the cost of their insurance. Any safety gain you might offer jurors, they now believe, provides too little utility and comes at too high a price. Jurors who already view their world as a safe place to live have nothing to gain from your client's lawsuit; they stand only to lose.

Loss framing allows jurors to see that a defense verdict will in fact create a loss for the whole community. Ruling for the defendant requires a choice to lower the existing safety standards in the community, making the defendant's negligent conduct acceptable. But that threatens the safety of everyone. It is the defendant that seeks to victimize the community by asking jurors to excuse conduct that was a radical departure from the norm, motivated solely by profit. The way to avoid the loss of the community's existing level of safety is to rule for the plaintiff—to maintain the status quo. Jurors who realize that they stand to lose their current level of safety, as well as their peace of mind, will be more willing to maintain the status quo by ruling for your client and against the defendant.

For example, Lazarus has consulted on several medical negligence cases in Boston and San Diego. Focus-group respondents in half a dozen or so cases from both areas have said at the start of almost every focus group that they were proud of their cities being at the forefront of medical care and science. Lazarus successfully framed all of these cases by acknowledging and buying into or embracing the high quality of health care, not just in the area, but at the defendant hospitals. The plaintiffs' cases were framed around what jurors needed to do to maintain that very high standard.

Bottom Up Case Preparation

Cusimano and Wenner developed the Jury Bias Model with the intent that trial lawyers would begin to analyze their cases with the five juror biases in mind. They would apply the Jury Bias Model's Ten Commandments to overcome those biases and achieve better trial results. What we discovered as a team, however, is that we did not have articulated step-by-step instructions to help trial lawyers visualize how the entire process works. It was as if we had given folks a list of the ingredients they'd need for making chili, but we hadn't spelled out all the directions.

That is why we developed Bottom Up case preparation. We wanted to give trial lawyers an assured, systematic process that, if followed—along with some help from us in interpretation— would provide the best possible results for their clients. Bottom Up case preparation is empirically based. You begin by researching the mindsets of likely jurors and build on that. Too often, talented and intuitive lawyers describe their cases to us based on their own understanding of the world or on the advice of their experts. Victims of "naive realism," trial lawyers believe that their jurors will see the evidence the same way they do.[30]

But in real-world practice, we have learned that jurors and trial lawyers often have widely diverging ideas of what a case is actually about. So, we decided to start with where the jurors are and construct the case from the beginning based on a trial story that is consistent with jurors' beliefs. Bottom Up case preparation thus combines the hard science we developed in our research for the Jury Bias Model with the hard facts about the way your likely jurors will view your particular case. We don't know of a better, more effective way to prepare a case for trial.

WHAT WE HAVE LEARNED

In order to combat the five biases of the Jury Bias Model, you must familiarize yourself with the Jury Bias Model's Ten Commandments—counteractive measures that combat those biases:

1. Compose a trial story.
2. Elicit confirmation.
3. Remember that beliefs persevere.
4. Sequence the available evidence.
5. Heed the norm.
6. Reverse the fundamental attribution error.
7. Plan for the hindsight bias.
8. Create empathy.
9. Drop the anchor.
10. Build the frame.

---

[30] *See* Lee Ross and Andrew Ward, "Naive Realism in Everyday Life: Implications for Social Conflict and Misunderstanding," in *Values and Knowledge*, eds. Edward S. Reed, Elliot Turiel, and Terrance Brown (Mahwah, NJ: Laurence Erlbaum Associates, 1996), 103–135.

Bottom Up case preparation gives you a consistent framework for applying the hard science of our Jury Bias Model to the individual facts of your particular case. By preparing your case from the bottom up, you begin with the beliefs your jurors already have and build your case from the start with a trial story that's consistent with those beliefs.

The next chapter will discuss the differences between Bottom Up and top-down case preparation.

3

BOTTOM UP™ VERSUS TOP-DOWN CASE PREPARATION

What is the difference between Bottom Up case preparation and the traditional approach to preparing a case for trial? The traditional system, the way virtually all lawyers are trained, is the top-down, or TOGA, approach (Top-down, Object-based, Goal-oriented Approach).[1] Both methods are strategies for sequencing, ordering, and processing information. Both are used in a wide spectrum of applications in addition to trial preparation, including software development, the hard and soft sciences, and even coaching.

---

[1] Adam Maria Gadomski, "Human Organization Socio-Cognitive Vulnerability: the TOGA Meta-Theory Approach to the Modeling Methodology," *International Journal of Critical Infrastructures* 5 (2009): 120–155.

TOP-DOWN CASE PREPARATION

The traditional approach to case preparation has you begin with the law as you expect it to be and then has you fill in the facts to prove the elements of the case. Clients visit your office and you ask a series of questions to learn their version of the facts. But the whole time your clients are talking, you are thinking, "What causes of action would I file in this case?" If you think it's a negligence case, you ask questions targeting the four elements of that cause of action: duty, breach of duty, proximate cause, and damages. You focus on a different set of elements in a premises liability case, and yet another in a product liability case.

You immediately begin organizing and processing the facts as they relate to the law, asking yourself questions. Which cause or causes of action fit these facts? Are there enough facts to satisfy the most difficult element of that claim for relief? You think down the road to the law in the jury charge and the evidence you would need to support the jury's verdict and sustain it on appeal.

That's the way lawyers are trained from the time they enter law school. Spot as many legal issues as possible. Look for the challenges in the case and decide how to overcome them. Find experts to pinpoint what the defendant did wrong—a protocol the doctor failed to adhere to or a warning the manufacturer chose not to provide. Once you outline the legal steps, you conduct discovery to find the facts that fit with what your expert told you your case is about.

Top-down case preparation relies on top-down logic—deductive reasoning. For example: It is negligent for restaurants to serve coffee so hot that it scalds customers when spilled. McDonald's sold coffee that gave third-degree burns to an elderly woman. McDonald's was negligent. Under the traditional approach, you line up that syllogism, plug in your evidence, and think you are ready to prepare for the trial itself: voir dire, opening, direct, cross, the jury charges and instructions, and closing.

Bottom Up™ Case Preparation

Bottom Up case preparation is different. Of course, you still need to know the applicable law in your case and how the facts support it. But that is not where you start. Bottom Up case preparation relies on inductive and abductive reasoning, testing out different observations and theories, and knowing that the ultimate conclusion is uncertain. Listening to what the jurors think is important, not what you think is important, is the core of the process. When you know what matters to the jurors, you can position your case to match their thinking as much as possible. As we all know, that McDonald's hot coffee case would be awfully hard to successfully try today—no matter how straightforward it seems—using a top-down approach based solely on deductive logic.

Bottom Up case preparation begins by asking how the decision makers—the judge, jury, adjuster, or defense counsel—would react to a given set of facts. Would that change if you presented the facts in a different way? What kind of expert would be persuasive to jurors? What would the expert need to say to demonstrate that her opinions are in sync with the beliefs the jurors already have about how the harm occurred? When something in your trial story is inconsistent with what your jurors already believe, it creates what psychologist Jean Piaget termed *cognitive disequilibrium*—the inability to fit new information into our existing schemas.[2] Trying to process inconsistent experiences causes anxiety and confusion. It is much easier to find out which way the river is flowing and paddle your canoe in that direction.

Bottom Up case preparation is an active process of looping back and forth between the facts, the case core, and the trial story, and of discovering schema, developing ideas, and testing them against the research and data. It requires you to revise your

---

[2] J. Piaget, *The Essential Piaget*, eds. H.E. Gruber and J.J. Voneche (New York: Basic Books, 1977).

case core and rework your trial story if necessary. If you test that out with focus groups and it's still not right, you rebuild again.

Bottom Up™ Case Preparation

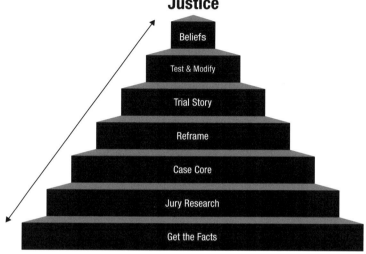

Bottom Up™ case preparation is really just a step-by-step approach to help trial lawyers apply the tools we developed in the Jury Bias Model to their own cases. It allows trial lawyers to understand the process and to adapt it for smaller cases that might not warrant an investment in a series of focus groups.

YOUR OWN WORST ENEMY

Lawyers often need help from someone not steeped in the case, someone with a knowledgeable objective view. In today's environment, that would be an experienced trial consultant. Lawyers think like lawyers, reason like lawyers, and prepare like lawyers. "We have met the enemy, and it is us."[3] Lawyers tend to complicate things, and they have great difficulty in determining

---

[3] A quote from *Pogo*, the title and central character of a long-running daily comic strip created by Walt Kelly (1913–1973).

how to strip down a message to its core. And trial lawyers fall prey to their own intuitions. Like anyone else, lawyers believe they see the world as it really is. But trial lawyers are governed by the same biases and errors in decision-making as everyone else. As a result, trial lawyers who assume that jurors will agree with their perception of a case are taking a big gamble. In fact, in virtually every focus group that any of us conduct, we learn something new and find ourselves surprised by the focus-group respondents' reactions to some aspect of the facts.

PROCESS, NOT FORMULA

Bottom Up case preparation is a rigorous process, but it is not a formula. There is no single answer or magic incantation for every lawsuit. Every plaintiff has different needs. Every fact pattern is different. Every jurisdiction is different.

And every lawyer is different in how she can best process and assimilate information to present a case in a unique way. Understanding our process and the science that underlies it will help you apply and adapt it to the unique circumstances of each case you take.

Because Bottom Up case preparation is a comprehensive process, you can apply it in every phase of case preparation in any type of lawsuit. Others have already provided trial lawyers with excellent resources for incorporating various heuristics in specific aspects of case preparation. The widely regarded *Reptile*[4] teaches one way (out of several) to use heuristics to the plaintiff's advantage. Rick Friedman and Patrick Malone's excellent

---

[4] Don Keenan and David Ball, *Reptile: The 2009 Manual of the Plaintiff's Revolution* (Balloon Press, 2009).

Rules of the Road[5]—useful in nearly any case—explains how to develop trial strategies predicated on the norm bias, the subject of our fifth commandment. And equally valuable is Mark Mandell's remarkable *Case Framing*, which powerfully, and much more broadly, illustrates the subject of our tenth commandment concerning how best to frame each issue in your case for maximizing results in trial, mediation, and depositions.[6]

The process of Bottom Up case preparation is a more comprehensive approach. With its emphasis on jury research and constantly revisiting the facts, it requires dedication and work to get through it. The whole process works best when you invest the time to truly understand the science underlying it. We love it when our clients ask us, "Why would that work?" or "What's that based on?"

Time changes, juries change, circumstances change, and you must be flexible enough to change as well. Inevitably, there are times in trial when a witness says something unexpected or when something unanticipated happens. If you're simply following someone else's formula, it's difficult to deal with a sudden change. But when you've invested the time to understand the emotional and cognitive biases and errors in decision-making that we're all prone to, you're better able to improvise when you need to. Lawyers who make the effort ultimately reach a satisfying level of confidence. They are prepared to present the case in the best, most effective way possible. They are able to meet the moment in

[5] Rick Friedman and Patrick Malone, *Rules of the Road* (Portland: Trial Guides, 2010).

[6] Mark Mandell, *Case Framing* (Portland: Trial Guides, 2015).

trial that so often comes without warning. They understand that there is no formulaic silver bullet that hits the target in every case.

From our perspective, it's the difference between memorizing something and learning it. When Cusimano was in law school, he posted this on his mirror: "To understand is to know." When you understand something, you don't have to try to remember it. You own it. That's the approach we took in developing the Jury Bias Model twenty years ago, and it's what we're endeavoring to teach now with Bottom Up case preparation. We will spend the next six chapters teaching you the Bottom Up case preparation method.

WHAT WE HAVE LEARNED

Bottom Up case preparation is a different process from the traditional top-down approach. Top-down case preparation begins with the ultimate legal issues you anticipate facing at trial and then searches out facts to support what your experts suggest you'll need to prove.

Bottom Up case preparation begins with what the decision makers think is important, not what you or your experts think is important. Once you know that, you can tailor your case to fit those expectations as closely as possible. Without that understanding, lawyers are their own worst enemies. They believe that the rest of the world will see their cases just as they do, but this is rarely true.

Finally, Bottom Up case preparation is a process, not a formula. You can use the process in every case, but what you do with what you learn will be different in every case because every case is different. Memorizing a formula is not the answer. The answer is to understand the process and the science that underlies it.

4

INVESTIGATING
THE FACTS

Investigating the facts is the first step in Bottom Up case preparation. And it should be; facts are your best friend. Treat them like it. Think about your relationship with your best friend—the friend you have known since childhood. Did you check in once with your friend when you first met each other, and never check back to see if anything had changed, or do you check in periodically? Has your relationship evolved over time, or is it still the same as it was when you were children? Do you see your friend the same way today, through the same lens, or has your view of your friend changed as you have both gained new life experiences and reordered your priorities over time?

Most attorneys study the facts early in the case and take them as they are, viewing them as static. Instead, you should start with the facts and never leave them. The facts themselves don't change, but what focus-group respondents tell us over and over again is that the relationship of the facts to each other will change as you change the order and the frame in which you present the facts. You should constantly revisit the facts to learn what order and what frame give you the strongest trial story. By reordering the evidence, you can greatly increase the power of good facts, discover some seemingly insignificant facts that help, and minimize the negative impact of bad facts.

LEGAL PROOF VERSUS JURY PROOF

Focus-group responses can teach you what other facts, which you didn't think to ask about or investigate originally, might be helpful to your case. Often, facts arise that you can put into evidence, facts that you might never have thought of because they are not absolutely required in order to meet the minimum level of proof of your cause of action. In other words, these facts are not the facts you need to survive summary judgement, nor are they part of what we call *legal proof,* but they may be an important part of the trial story.

Focus-group respondents (and jurors) often want to know about information that, while it might not prove the case legally, will make all the difference in how jurors understand the evidence that does decide the case. This information is what we call *jury proof.* You are likely to lose your case without adequate jury proof, regardless of the amount of legal proof you have. Too many lawyers disregard jury proof because of their training in how to present the best legal proof.

One of the biggest reasons we advocate using early focus groups is because they allow attorneys time during discovery to investigate the facts jurors want to know.[1] After discovery is closed, it doesn't do much good to learn that jurors are interested in information you never thought to ask about. But if you learn

---

[1] We have used focus groups in cases for some of our clients even before they decided to take the case, as a tool to understand the case's potential and its pitfalls before making a major commitment.

early in the process what additional information is critical to jurors, you can pursue it during discovery and build this essential information into your trial story.

As an illustration, consider the case of a pregnant woman who slipped and fell on a wet floor in a pet store. The facts of the case are as follows:

> An aquarium had been leaking. Despite the manager noting the problem and instructing an employee to clean it up, the floor was never mopped or dried. Nor was there any signage or warning. The woman thought she was okay when she got up from her fall, but started having cramps when she left the store.

Those facts establish legal proof of a breach on the part of the pet store that resulted in the customer slipping and getting hurt. But based on those facts, focus-group respondents did not find the pet store liable. Why? The personal-responsibility and blame-the-plaintiff biases. Focus-group respondents relied on their preexisting biases and blamed the woman for not taking proper care, especially since she knew she was pregnant and should have been particularly cautious to protect both herself and her unborn child.

However, there are other facts in this case. It turns out that when the woman asked to use the pet store's phone to call her husband to come pick her up, the store manager refused because of corporate policy. The woman had to borrow a cell phone from another customer in the store to make her call. She didn't feel very well, so she asked the store manager if she could sit down near the front of the store while she waited. The manager told her he preferred it if she sat in the pet grooming room in the back of the store and led her to that area. The store manager's behavior, when included as part of the trial story, changed the jurors' willingness to find against the defendant in the case. Without this jury proof, the facts that were so critically and legally important to the standing of the claim were sterile and insufficient to the jurors.

The jury proof in this case is a lens through which people view the corporation. If the jurors think the manager is the kind of person who would behave that way toward a pregnant woman who slipped and fell, it is human nature and much easier for them to find the manager, and therefore the store, liable than if they view the store manager as a good person with a kind heart.

These kinds of perceptions can be critical to winning a case with a jury. Failure to examine the kind of information jurors want to know about because you are myopically focused on the legal elements of the cause of action is a failure to revisit the facts and reexamine how the story elements fit together. Focus groups are a critical tool in this process.

Lawyers tend to take a very narrow view of their cases. They are trained to think in terms of the breach of duty, the causation, and the damages. And lawyers often use experts to narrow the view of a case even more. Instead, you should give jurors a broader view of the case, so they can better understand what happened in context, just as they understand things that happen in their daily lives.

In their daily lives, jurors would not ask what the duty of the pet store was to the pregnant woman; nor would they ask if the duty was breached, if that breach constituted cause for harm, and what the damages were. That is not the way people think. They say, "Are you kidding me? A woman fell and she's pregnant and you won't let her use your phone? You won't let her sit down on your chair? What kind of person does that?" That manager is not the kind of person the jury is going to root for. Discovering the jury proof in your case is critical.

Ignoring "Unrelated" Facts Can Kill Your Case

Trial consultants always tell plaintiffs' attorneys that the case needs to be about the defendant's conduct, not about the plaintiff's conduct. Although it's important, plaintiffs don't win cases by establishing what great people the plaintiff and her family are, how tragic their loss is, and how their lives have been irreparably changed. Plaintiffs win cases by getting jurors to focus on the defendant and the defendant's conduct. Yes, it is important to show that the plaintiff is a responsible person, but not necessarily in the first part of the case.

So how can it be a mistake for a plaintiff in a nursing home case to focus all attention on the conduct of the orderly who hit one elderly resident with enough force that there was blood on the wall next to the resident's bed? For the legal proof, all one needs to know is the orderly's history—which includes previous episodes of abusing nursing home residents, the physical abuse the orderly inflicted on the plaintiff, and the harm and damages the abuse caused.

Yet just as plaintiffs win cases by focusing jurors' attention on the conduct of the defendants, defendants often win cases by focusing jurors' attention on the conduct of the plaintiffs and the plaintiffs' families, especially in situations where the plaintiffs or their family members could have taken some action to prevent (or not taken an action that contributed to) the harm the plaintiffs are suffering. In this case, as in most nursing home cases, one of the first questions focus-group respondents ask (and, therefore, one of the most important pieces of information jurors want to know) is how often the abused resident's children visited her in the nursing home. Failing to include that background cripples the plaintiff's chance at recovery.[2]

At the time we started working on this case, trial was weeks away. In the focus groups we conducted, respondents asked how frequently the plaintiff's son visited her. Though he was well prepared with every aspect of the case against the nursing home—the orderly's record, the ways in which the nursing home could have and should have known of the orderly's history, and other violations by the nursing home—one piece of information the attorney did not have as part of the trial story was how often the resident's children visited her. The attorney was so focused on making sure he had everything he needed to focus the case on the defendant's misconduct, he had not taken the time to collect the jury proof that would decide this case.

Absent information confirming that the resident's son had come to visit her regularly, focus-group participants decided during their deliberations that the son was just involved in the case for the money. The participants thought his failure to visit his mother in the nursing home showed he clearly did not care about her well-being. Further, had he taken the time to visit her regularly, he would have seen the conditions in the home and would have had the chance to move her to a better facility.

Therefore, while the actions of the orderly and the nursing home were abominable, these respondents could not find for the plaintiff because the entire problem could have been avoided had the son not shown such callous disregard for his mother. In the eyes of these respondents, the entire lawsuit was simply about the son seeing his mother's misfortune as a meal ticket. After all, they thought, the son likely saw no other attributes in his mother, given his conduct. (This is another example of the suspicion bias at work.)

---

[2] At least assuming the plaintiff's children did visit her regularly.

Don't Wait until It's Too Late

Waiting too long to do focus groups is one of the biggest mistakes we see attorneys make. Attorneys simply can't investigate the facts properly without early research into what facts jurors will find important. Attorneys can easily prepare the facts that go into the legal proof, but the facts that make up the jury proof tend not to reveal themselves without focus groups or other research tools that illuminate what jurors want to know and will find important about the case.

Attorneys often wait too long to do focus groups on a significant case because their own optimism about the case leads them to believe that it will settle. Most lawyers can't help but think that most of the cases they have taken are good cases. After all, why would an attorney invest time and money in a case in which she does not have confidence? But often a case, even a very good case, does not deserve the level of confidence it has achieved in the attorney's mind. After all, even the best case has problems, and even the best plaintiff has his faults.

Yet as the attorney invests time and energy in the case, it is hard (if not impossible) to maintain objectivity.[3] Instead, the attorney's outrage over the defendant's wrongdoing grows, desire for justice for the client boils over, and confidence rises. Even when attorneys are able to maintain a sense of objectivity, the

---

[3] It is this difficulty to maintain objectivity that causes us to recommend against attorneys conducting their own focus groups. While the practice has become more and more common, we have serious concerns given an attorney's job is to be an advocate for her client. It is hard to be a professional advocate for your clients on a full-time basis and suddenly switch to the role of dispassionate research facilitator. When we review recordings with attorneys who have done their own focus groups, the attorneys often don't see their lack of objectivity even when we point it out to them. Presenting facts to focus groups in a biased way, even if the bias is unintentional or subtle, can often be worse than not doing a focus group at all.

reality is that the overwhelming majority of cases with reasonable and legitimate claims settle.

Some attorneys think there is no need to assume the extra cost of focus groups for a case they are reasonably certain will settle. Except, of course, for the fact that when the case doesn't settle, the attorney has to engage in a last-minute scramble to figure out how best to present the case at trial.

In our experience, it is more prudent to think of focus groups not as preparation for trial, but as a way to strengthen your case in any forum. Being able to tell the best story in the most persuasive fashion helps not only in front of a jury, but also in front of a mediator, an insurance adjuster, opposing counsel, and the judge.[4] The techniques for doing appropriate research and applying the findings to your case are not designed to understand and influence jury decision-making; they are techniques designed to understand and influence *human* decision-making. The science applies to the way human beings are wired to make decisions. Mediators, insurance adjusters, opposing counsel, and judges are all human beings—just like jurors. The elements that make a story more compelling to a jury also make the story more compelling to any other audience you have along the way.

The better prepared you are with a persuasive case, the more success you will have in reaching a good settlement. Using focus groups to investigate the facts, understanding the best way to arrange those facts and their relationships to each other, and understanding the best way to present your case is not an exercise just for a jury trial. It is an integral part of achieving greater success as a litigator. In any case with significant value, you should seriously consider bringing on a consultant to conduct focus groups.

---

[4] In addition to having prepared clients for successful bench trials in the United States, we are doing more and more cases in Canada, where bench trials are much more common than jury trials. There, we use focus groups in anticipation of the fact that if the case doesn't settle we will try it before a judge.

Although there are resources in the marketplace on how to conduct your own focus groups, there are many risks associated with that decision. As a result, the three of us who are attorneys don't do focus groups on our own cases, but depend on others. The rare exceptions to this have been focus groups to determine whether to even take a case.

THE PARADOX OF GOOD FACTS

One of the ironies of having an excellent case with strong facts is it can cause an attorney to prepare less well than he might if the case had more contested issues. In addition to being over-confident that the case will settle (see above), we see attorneys with strong engineering, scientific, or medical evidence fall into the trap of relying on that strong evidence to carry the case. Worse still is when we hear what great experts the plaintiff has to explain the power of the "incontrovertible" evidence in the case. Paradoxically, the stronger the evidence is, the weaker the lawyer's trial story often is.

When attorneys rely on slam-dunk evidence and outstanding experts, they are preparing a case that relies on experts and science, engineering, or medicine. One problem with this approach is that it rests the plaintiff's case on an area in which the defendant is an expert. In a medical negligence case, the defendant is a medical expert. In a product liability case, the defendant is the one who employs engineers or scientists every day. In either of these cases, the plaintiff is a layperson with no specific knowledge of the medicine, science, or engineering. Yet the plaintiff is bringing a claim against a defendant who *is* an expert in the field. In order to give the plaintiff's claim credibility, the plaintiff's attorney brings in paid experts, whose job it is to duel the defendant and the defense experts on a field that is already tilted toward the defendant. When you make the case about the experts and the science, engineering, or medicine, you fight the battle on terrain that favors the defendant.

But more germane to the discussion of how to investigate, revisit, and reorder the facts is that the main problem with making your case about the experts and the science is that jurors seldom decide the outcome based on the experts and the science. Jurors decide the outcome based on the story behind the facts.[5] We don't want our case to be one of dueling experts. Yes, we have to neutralize the natural advantage the defendant has, but we can't stop there. Neutralizing the defendant's natural advantage results in a tie; a tie results in sustaining the status quo. The status quo is generally a defense verdict—unless you have successfully implemented loss framing, as we explained earlier.

A case that rests on experts and strong scientific evidence often never gets to the story. In the end, it is the story about how the facts come together that determines the ordering of the facts, and the sweep of the story introducing the human element that results in jurors rejecting a status quo that favors the defendant and, instead, taking action for the plaintiff. Plaintiffs need juries to take an action—to do something. Which means plaintiffs need to focus on the story—how the facts fit together—in order to achieve success. Facts and evidence are important and necessary. But facts alone seldom sustain a successful plaintiff's case.

---

[5] Our research reveals that jurors believe that paid expert witnesses are not as credible as other witnesses.

FIND THE STORY
BEHIND THE FACTS

When we talk about investigating the facts, we really are talking about finding the story behind the facts. Facts by themselves can be dry and dull. The arc of every popular love story, even every great love story, boils down to one or the other of the following sets of facts: boy meets girl, boy and girl fall in love, boy and girl live happily ever after (*Sleepless in Seattle*, *When Harry Met Sally*); or the more classic and tragic version where boy meets girl, boy and girl fall in love, social or personal upheaval rips boy and girl apart (*Romeo and Juliet*, *Love Story*, *Titanic*, *Casablanca*). If your case is a love story, your success does not rest in the facts.

Your success rests in telling the story around the facts. When we investigate the facts, we are trying to understand the story behind the facts so we can better assemble the individual pieces in the most compelling and persuasive order. Focus groups reveal which facts are most important and why. More important, focus groups reveal the story behind the facts that allows you to order, emphasize, and explain the relationships between the facts in the most compelling way.

FACTS IN FOCUS

Understanding the story behind the facts and how they fit together allows you to understand how to frame your case. Even the most basic references we make to a case convey information about what we think of it and what we want or expect others to think of it, and can influence the outcome.

Earlier in this chapter, you read about a case involving a pregnant woman who slipped on a puddle in a pet shop. How would you characterize that case? What is the first caption that comes to mind as you think about the case? No doubt, you shorthand that case to a *slip and fall*. And in doing so, as you convey information about the case to others, you are conveying an entire load of preconditioning information to those who hear you talk about the slip and fall case.

As far as most jurors are concerned, slip and fall cases are frivolous lawsuits brought by people who won't take responsibility for their own mistakes or stupidity. After all, a person has to be clumsy enough to slip (or trip) in order to be the plaintiff in a slip and fall case. Or worse yet, and just as likely in jurors' minds, they have to be conniving enough to see an opportunity to cash in by pretending or intending to slip so they can bring a claim against the innocent victim, the proprietor of the property on which they decided to fall.

If you recall the case described earlier in this chapter, the plaintiff did not win her slip and fall case because the negligence of the proprietor caused her to slip and fall. What the focus-group respondents told us was she won despite the fact that she made a (legally appropriate but jury inappropriate) slip and fall claim against a negligent proprietor. The plaintiff prevailed because the proprietor was a total jerk in ways that had nothing to do with the negligence that caused injury to the plaintiff. There were other (unimportant in the legal definition) facts that altered the way jurors viewed this case. Without these other legally unimportant facts, the plaintiff would never have overcome the stigma of making a slip and fall claim.

A narrow lesson to take from this is to always find other facts to bolster your slip and fall claim. A broader and more important lesson would be to learn how to reframe your cases. Unfortunately, the social stigma associated with the term "slip and fall" (much like "whiplash" or "hostile workplace") puts any plaintiff behind when making an associated claim. Regardless of the merit of a case, jurors come into some cases and, upon just hearing a short case description, assume the claim is frivolous or trumped up.

In another case we refer to as the Mega Mart case, the plaintiff slipped on the wet floor of a big-box retailer on a rainy day. She did not initially realize how seriously she was hurt, and she did not report the injury when it happened. It was only after she was home that she realized the fall had hurt her back.

In our focus groups, the case was seemingly unwinnable once group members knew it was a slip and fall. Respondents assumed the claim was bogus because the plaintiff got up and went home without telling anyone what happened. In respondents' minds, it was only after she got home that she realized she had missed out on a chance to sue for millions, so she made up the injury in order to make a claim. In other focus groups on the same case, we changed the facts to learn what the reaction would be. We learned that a customer who slipped and fell and didn't get up, complaining of pain and seeking assistance immediately, was just faking it so she could bring a suit for millions of dollars against the retailer. According to the focus-group participants, no matter what that plaintiff did on the day she fell, she would be unable to convince jurors that her injury was real and her claim was valid.

The problem is in the framing. A slip and fall case carries an anti-plaintiff frame. Among the things we learned from focus-group respondents was that they expected a large national retailer to have a protocol for dealing with slippery and wet floors on rainy days. They expected the national retailer to have some kind of training manual or video for employees to follow to make sure the floors are dry and safe—if for no other reason than to prevent frivolous lawsuits like this one from coming along. Somewhat ironically, therefore, jurors assume it is not possible for a customer to slip and fall due to anything other than the customer's own negligence.

But when we changed the way the story was framed so it was not a slip and fall case, the plaintiff's prospects changed. A case about "maintaining a dangerous condition for customers" or a case about "bad supervision" or "bad management" simply retooled the way jurors thought about the case. It changed the lens through which jurors saw and thought about the issues in the case. So instead of presenting a case where a woman slipped on a wet floor on a rainy day, we could present a case where a store manager ignored protocol and training, and employees ignored a dangerous situation, resulting in the injury that the protocol was designed to prevent, had it been followed.

Focusing not only on the facts, but also on the focus-group respondents' expectations about what was appropriate, led to a new way to frame the case such that the same facts would appear in a different light. That is what we mean by investigating the facts and never leaving them.

WHAT WE HAVE LEARNED

Get the Facts

Get the Facts

Step one in the Bottom Up case preparation method is to get the facts. Our research and experiences have persuaded us of the following:

♦ The way each fact impacts your case is not static. Each individual fact is the same when viewed on its own. But taken together, the facts bring different meaning based on their order, what is included, what is excluded, and how they are framed.

◆ Investigate early. Don't wait until it's too late in your case to conduct focus groups that teach you which facts are important, what facts you need to find to fill in the gaps, which order makes your facts easiest to understand, how your facts relate to each other, and how to frame them.

◆ Investigate often. Don't ever assume you are done learning about the facts in your case. Revisit your facts, your story order, what to include, what to exclude, and your frame to make certain you aren't leaving anything out or missing any key points to your story.

◆ Commit to understanding all of the files in your office and where, when, and how you will investigate and reexamine the case, the frame, and the story order. Rather than having to scramble at the last minute to prepare a case for trial, be ready to present the best case you can because you've assumed none of your cases will settle. Reexamine the case facts and reframe the cases periodically, and you will improve the settlement values of your cases in the process.

5

CONDUCTING
JURY RESEARCH

Why is jury research so important that it forms the second step in our Bottom Up process for case preparation? Because without jury research, trial lawyers tend to prepare cases based on intuition and their own views of the world. They become persuaded by expensive expert opinions, compromising corporate documents, and earnest and articulate lay witnesses who line up beside their clients. Lawyers develop their own specific ideas of what the most compelling trial story looks like and that's all they see.

They forget who they're talking to, although they should know better. If you were asked to speak at your Aunt Edna's retirement center, you might not open with your very favorite joke—even if the guys in your poker group think it's hilarious. You would consider your audience. That's what early jury research is all about.

When you use focus groups to conduct jury research early in your case, you may learn that your case is not at all about what you think it is. The critical fact(s) for jurors may be something completely unimportant to your legal analysis. Or you may uncover a stumbling block for jurors that you never would have imagined. In either instance, you're back to the drawing board to create a trial story that's persuasive for jurors—not for you. The earlier you begin jury research, the sooner you can begin preparing a case that works.

What should you be looking for in your jury research? Land mines—in every aspect of the case. Early in the lawsuit, search for jurors' conscious and unconscious attitudes about all sides of the case. Work to uncover the anti-plaintiff biases described in the Jury Bias Model:[1]

1. Suspicion
2. Victimization
3. Personal Responsibility
4. Stuff Happens
5. Blame the Plaintiff

You want to know what jurors think is important—even if, in your estimation, it's not. What preconceptions or misconceptions do potential jurors have about the subject matter of the case, the defendant, and the injuries or damages involved? Later in your case preparation, you should often focus on particular exhibits and witnesses to test whether they're persuasive.

These factors are often overlooked when lawyers prepare cases, as they focus instead on favorable facts or laws that seem as though they should be determinative. But jurors often fail to hear the testimony from a compelling expert witness because they've been waylaid by an anti-plaintiff bias or a random, wrongheaded notion about an important element in your case.

After conducting thousands of focus groups, we've learned that no part of effective case preparation is more important than early jury research. There is truth in the adage that "for those who believe, no proof is necessary. For those who do not believe, no proof is possible."

---

[1] *See* chapter 1, "The Jury Bias Model Part One," page 15.

Focus Groups

Several tools exist for conducting effective jury research. Of these, focus groups are without question the most useful resource for understanding jurors' perceptions and beliefs about your case. Whenever possible, we recommend conducting more than one focus group to ensure that you understand the attitudes you'll face at trial and that you've developed an effective trial story that builds on them. There are two main types of focus groups, though it's sometimes helpful to combine elements from both.

The Concept Focus Group

The gold standard for jury research is the concept focus group, especially when you do it early in a case. This is because the entire purpose of a concept focus group is to learn what jurors think and believe about your case.

In a concept focus group, you present the facts to a group of laypeople to learn how they intuitively understand the story. It's a sort of conversation in which you learn how they process the facts. How do they perceive the plaintiff and the defendant in the case? What unconscious attitudes do they demonstrate toward each side and toward events in the case? Which facts do they attach great importance to (*overweighting*) and which facts play little part in their view of the case (*underweighting*)?

For instance, in a breast cancer case we discuss several times in this book, the plaintiff went to her family doctor with a lump in her breast. In the many concept focus groups that Wenner and Cusimano conducted, they asked, "What would you expect the doctor to do?" The responses were many and varied:

"When I went to my doctor, this is what he did . . ."

"The doctor should order a biopsy."

"The doctor should get an ultrasound."

"She should have a mammogram."

"How long had she been his patient? Did the doctor know her history? Did he get her family history?"

To every response, Wenner and Cusimano's reply was some variation of "That's interesting. Tell me more about that. What makes you curious to know that? What makes that important to you?" In this way, they slowly elicited the group members' responses to each of the facts. This is how you learn which facts potential jurors will overweight and which they will underweight. You keep asking questions until you understand not just what they think, but why what they think is important to them.

Once you know the facts jurors are likely to overweight, you can construct the trial story to emphasize the ones that are good for your case. If you're fortunate and jurors underweight facts that are harmful to your case, you weave in those facts in a way that makes them even less consequential. When you discover the opposite—that jurors overweight facts that hurt your case—find a way to reframe those facts so the jurors focus on something else entirely. The critical point is that you cannot know how to build your case in a way that's consistent with jurors' beliefs unless you do the jury research early on—and preferably with concept focus groups.

You can also use concept focus groups to test specific videos, photographs, different arguments, and so on. It is easy to make the mistake of relying on an animation, for example, because it cost so much to produce it. But the cost of using an animation or other demonstrative that doesn't advance your case is often much higher than the cost of leaving that expensive animation in your office unused.

We prefer to conduct at least two concept groups in order to compare different approaches and story orders, as well as to confirm findings from one group to the other. Because the order in which these questions and topics come up can have a significant impact on the conclusions focus-group participants reach, we change the order in which we present information between groups. We can compare the thought processes and patterns in the two groups to understand how the order of evidence and the story order can alter the outcome at trial.

THE STRUCTURED FOCUS GROUP

Once we have developed a research-based trial story and story order, structured focus groups are a useful tool for assessing them. You can think of structured focus groups as miniature mock trials. In a structured focus group, we present *clopenings*—short opening statements/closing arguments that lay out the case, highlight key evidence, draw conclusions, and argue for a verdict—from different attorneys playing opposite roles in the case. We then give respondents a brief set of instructions and watch them deliberate. When their deliberations are complete, we discuss their reactions and conclusions in a group setting.

The purpose of the structured focus group is to test the trial story you've developed. If you win, you know that you're on the right track. If you lose, you need to review what you learned from watching the deliberations, debriefing the respondents, and analyzing their answers to questionnaires. Often, the information you get from a structured focus group is narrower in scope than what you receive from a concept focus group. Use structured focus groups to test and then modify your trial story until you know you have it right—it's not unlike modifying your golf swing after a lesson from a pro.

With Bottom Up case preparation, we like to use both types of focus groups. Early on in a case, we conduct jury research by using concept focus groups to root out specific anti-plaintiff biases, learn what jurors think is important, and discover their thoughts and beliefs about the case. Later on, after we've developed the case core and trial story, we try them out on the structured focus group. That's when we learn whether our trial story or some other particular aspect of the case will actually resonate with the jury.

THE HYBRID FOCUS GROUP

Sometimes a case calls for a focus group that falls somewhere on the continuum between a pure concept group and a pure structured group. There might be a particular aspect of your case that's posing a challenge, for example, and you need to uncover juror beliefs and test out a possible approach based on those beliefs. There are no hard and fast rules.

For example, suppose you need more information on a couple of issues that you can test in the abstract with a concept group before you perform the structured group. In a toxic waste spill, you may want to know focus-group members' views on whether the legal requirements placed on the defendant are fair or not. You can test this principle to discover their views without disclosing that the requirements are the law. Once done, you can modify and test a structured argument that is more consistent with their views.

OTHER TOOLS FOR CONDUCTING JURY RESEARCH

Although focus groups are undeniably the best way to conduct effective jury research early in a case, they are not the only way. Many other tools are available for learning what you need to know. By approaching your research several different ways, you have the opportunity to reproduce and validate the information and results you might have obtained through focus groups. The more validators you have, the more confidence you'll have that you know what to expect from your jurors and that your trial story is effective and consistent with jurors' existing beliefs.

The following is a list of tools we use for conducting jury research outside of a focus group:

- *Peer Research*: We research every national study or survey we can find that relates to issues in a case we're involved in.
- *The Media*: We scour newspapers, magazines, and the internet to learn what's available to jurors on a particular case and on relevant issues. We also read blog comments and letters to the editor to understand jurors' reactions to stories in the media. Then we analyze that media coverage and public response in comparison to similar issues we've previously dealt with in thousands of focus groups done in the past to see what's similar and what's different.
- *Similar Lawsuits*: We search for lawsuits involving similar issues filed in the same community. Then we turn to our peers who tried those cases to learn what was successful and what wasn't.
- *Online Focus Groups*: Online groups are a cost-effective way to conduct jury research. They are not as useful as in-person groups in which you sit around a table with a group of people

and discuss their views in a more natural setting. But online focus groups are a fraction of the cost, and they provide a great deal of value for the money.

◆ *Surveys*: We use surveys to help understand the relationships between jurors' demographics and attitudes and their predispositions about the issues and parties in case. As a cautionary note, however, we've discovered that there is no demographic silver bullet. It is far more effective to delve into jurors' attitudes than to hunt down a perfect demographic that doesn't exist. Surveys are very helpful in developing both supplemental juror questionnaires and questions to ask during oral voir dire.

◆ *Dial Testing*: In very significant, very large, and very complex litigation, we use dial tests. Dial tests are a great way to understand the impact of precise segments of presentations, videos, slides, openings, and other demonstratives. Respondents are all given a dial and instructed to turn their dial in one direction if the information they are hearing or seeing makes them more likely to support the plaintiff, and another direction if the information makes them more likely to support the defendant. Software reads the positions of each respondent's dial once every second, which means we can track changes in perceptions of the test material moment to moment. Sometimes we find that a great presentation or demonstrative is ruined by a single moment's flaw, or a weak demonstrative is strengthened by a single phrase or image. Obviously, with this kind of precision, we can easily make valuable changes not only to how we present the case but to how we present the supporting evidence and arguments.

◆ *Mock Trials*: Mock trials can teach us how jurors will respond to an attorney's opening, closing, or general style. How do they feel about key witnesses and experts? In a case a couple of years ago, we learned that the mock jurors hated our client's expert even though our client was certain the expert's testimony would be fatal for the defendant.

The best way to understand your jurors' biases and beliefs is to use some combination of these tools in addition to concept focus groups. Having several resources that all point to the same major issues will assure you a successful trial story that is built around the things your jurors already believe.

LEARNING FROM FOCUS GROUPS

When we conduct concept focus groups, we're looking for land mines that could sabotage the plaintiff's case. These land mines are generally one of two varieties. First, we look for things that are important *about* the jurors, primarily their anti-plaintiff biases. And second, we look for things that are important *to* the jurors, such as preconceptions or misconceptions about the events or injuries particular to the case. No matter how many focus groups we conduct—and we've done or studied thousands—we always learn something new. Jury research teaches you to work from actual data, not from assumptions.

USING FOCUS GROUPS TO DISCOVER JUROR BIASES

Trial lawyers must regularly confront the five anti-plaintiff biases mentioned earlier: suspicion, victimization, personal responsibility, stuff happens, and blame the plaintiff. In our focus groups, we've looked for—and found—them all. Only by understanding the particular biases that exist in your case do you have the opportunity to reframe the issues and defuse jurors' biases.

Suspicion

As we've discussed earlier, jurors are often suspicious anytime the plaintiff claims to have suffered injuries that she did not report immediately to the police, the defendant, or the doctor. Did she phone the police? Did she see a doctor right away? Did a third party or her lawyer put her up to the lawsuit? Legally, these questions are not determinative. But psychologically, they can be pivotal. The reality is, if you represent a plaintiff, jurors will be suspicious of your client regardless of the facts or the order of events.

Neck Injury from a Rear-End Collision

In one of the cases that we've used in our lectures,[2] focus-group respondents were suspicious of a driver with a serious neck injury. A high school wrestling coach had been rear-ended late one night at an intersection. The drivers didn't call the police and the plaintiff didn't go to the doctor until the next day when he realized his neck was hurt. These two circumstances made the focus-group members suspicious. People generally believe that when you don't call the police and you don't go straight to the doctor, you're not hurt. Lawyers often use jury research to develop testimony from biomechanical engineers to explain the unavoidable forces that a rear-end collision—even at low speeds—exerts on a driver's neck.

Back Injury from a Slip and Fall

Recall the Mega Mart case in which the plaintiff slipped on the wet floor of a big-box retailer on a rainy day. Embarrassed, the woman went home without saying anything. It wasn't until later that she realized the fall had injured her back. She waited until a couple of days after the fall to report her injury to the store. Slip and fall cases are almost guaranteed to arouse suspicion. We were not surprised to hear that concept focus-group members

---

[2] This case will be discussed again in chapter 7, "Developing the Trial Story" on page 147.

suspected the woman of taking two days to realize not that the fall hurt her back but that she could profit from her own clumsiness by suing the Mega Mart for her trumped up "injuries."

We can easily recall numerous car crash[3] and slip and fall cases where juror suspicions have revealed that there is no good time to go to the doctor or hire a lawyer. Knowing this going into a concept focus group gives you an opportunity to explore the group's reactions to other facts capable of directing jurors' attention away from the plaintiff's conduct and onto the defendant's. In the Mega Mart case, we accomplished that by reframing the case as one of bad management, where the store manager chose not to follow the retailer's procedures for customer safety on a rainy day.

Personal Responsibility

We've also used concept focus groups to uncover juror biases related to personal responsibility. Jurors are less likely to find a defendant responsible when they believe the plaintiff's conduct was irresponsible. Sometimes we're dazed when we discover exactly what jurors find to be careless.

Failure to Diagnose Breast Cancer

In the breast cancer case we've previously mentioned, Cusimano and Wenner conducted multiple focus groups involving the missed diagnosis.

A woman in her forties discovered a lump in her breast and consulted her family doctor. He sent her for a mammogram, which the radiologist interpreted as indeterminate and in need of follow-up testing. The family doctor relied on a physician's assistant and a nurse practitioner in his practice. The physician's assistant received the indeterminate results and filed

---

[3] We generally advise not to use the term *accident* as it implies that no one is at fault, and that is not what we are trying to prove.

them away as normal. When the patient telephoned a week later, she was told that the results were normal. A year later, the mass was much larger, and doctors made the cancer diagnosis.

In the focus groups Cusimano and Wenner conducted in this case, one surprising thing emerged: jurors blamed the plaintiff, not the doctor whose staff had told her that her mammogram was normal. One of the land mines was the sheer size of the lump. The first year, the lump was two to three centimeters, but by the second year, it had grown to three or four centimeters.

The focus-group respondents couldn't see past the size of the tumor, which was a predictor for whether the woman would survive. The respondents blamed the plaintiff.

What did she do wrong? She didn't challenge her doctor's opinion. Women in the focus groups claimed that they would have done research on the internet. They would have sought out a second opinion. They would have insisted on a biopsy. The plaintiff was irresponsible, said the focus-group respondents; she was to blame for dodging her personal responsibility for her own health.

Discovering these land mines in concept focus groups allowed Wenner and Cusimano to go back to the facts to find ways to divert focus from the plaintiff back to where it belonged—on the doctor's conduct. The doctor had streamlined procedures in his practice to allow him to make more money by seeing more patients. Under traditional systems, the doctor himself would have telephoned the patient or ensured she return to see him. But under the new system, which required less of the doctor's time and oversight, it was entirely foreseeable that what happened to the plaintiff could also happen to other patients. Effective jury research enabled Cusimano and Wenner to reframe the story successfully by focusing jurors' attention on different facts.

Officer Injured in Pursuit of Auto Thief

In a concept focus group that Lazarus conducted a couple of years ago, the plaintiff was a police officer injured during a high-speed chase by a product defect in the police car he was driving. Lazarus was shocked when the initial reaction from focus-group participants went something like this: "What's he doing in a high-speed chase over a stolen car? The police shouldn't be chasing after a car thief at seventy miles per hour down the streets."

That's exactly what we want from jury research—the kind of feedback we didn't anticipate. We were able to take that and turn it around to the plaintiff's benefit by framing the officer's conduct in terms of our shared need to live in a safe world. Police officers willing to pursue criminals in the act of grand theft provide us all with a safe community in which we know that our families and possessions are secure.

Blame the Plaintiff

None of the five juror biases is more sinister than the fifth—blame the plaintiff. Through numerous concept focus groups, we have learned that the blame-the-plaintiff bias imbues jurors with beliefs that are concerning and sometimes very creative.

Exploding Tennessee Vacation Rental

For an example of using a focus group to root out the blame-the-plaintiff bias, let's return to the case that Cusimano worked on with the vacation chalet that exploded during breakfast and slid down a mountain near Gatlinburg, Tennessee, while an elderly couple from Michigan was still inside. Cusimano thought the case was a slam dunk. It was the first time anyone had rented the brand-new house. The Michigan couple had spent just one night there. It was obvious that something was wrong in the construction or in a propane tank. How could anyone possibly blame the plaintiffs?

During the first concept focus group, the initial comment went like this: "North Carolina has tremors, and Gatlinburg is in the same geographic plane, so probably what happened is that a tremor shook the house overnight and caused a gas leak." But the rest of the comments were aimed squarely at the nice old couple on vacation from Michigan. One line of attack focused on the wife: "If they were cooking breakfast, she probably did something on the stove that caused the gas leak." The other targeted the husband: "The night before, the old man was fooling with the gas fireplace, and he did something to cause the leak."

We've seen a lot of variations on blame the plaintiff over the years, but Cusimano was taken aback. No one suggested that the tank was faulty or that construction was shabby. The focus-group respondents blamed the plaintiffs for sending a brand-new vacation rental sliding down the mountainside over breakfast.[4]

Failure to Diagnose Kidney Infection

The tendency of jurors to blame the plaintiff is so strong that you can incite jurors to it with a single ill-considered word choice. Wenner was involved in a case where a woman's physician failed to diagnose her kidney infection. Although the plaintiff had blood in her urine, her family practice doctor repeatedly prescribed antibiotics for a urinary tract infection (UTI). Unfortunately, she actually had severe kidney disease and had to undergo a kidney transplant. Had the disease been diagnosed earlier, she would not have lost her kidney.

During the plaintiff's lawyer's presentation to the focus group, he said that the doctor prescribed antibiotics "prophylactically" for what he thought were repeated UTIs. As Wenner watched from another room while the group deliberated, he was astonished. They speculated whether the husband caused the problem by

---

[4] To review how Cusimano addressed this issue, *see* "Sequence the Available Evidence" in chapter 2, page 51.

not using prophylactics when he and his wife had sex. Then they hypothesized that the wife was probably cheating on her husband with men who did not use prophylactics. All the while this sweet woman and her husband were watching as focus-group members seized upon the word "prophylactic" to blame the plaintiff.

This is also an example of the importance of using simple, clear, language. Why say "prophylactic" when "preventative" will work?

Trial Lawyers Are Guilty Too

Trial lawyers are not immune from the inclination to blame the plaintiff. When we make CLE presentations around the country, we often engage in an exercise that we are about to spoil for readers by describing it here. Before a break, we ask everyone to have a look outside at the landing because we'd read in the paper that someone fell from there just two months earlier. This fall is always pure fabrication on our part.

When our brothers and sisters in arms—fellow trial lawyers—reassemble, we ask for their ideas about what must have happened. "Someone had too much to drink," one trial lawyer usually volunteers. "I bet they were roughhousing," another will add. No one has ever suggested that the cause might be a structural problem with the staircase or railing. Yet these are the very people we would all expect to empathize with the plaintiff and to be attuned to the risks caused by negligence and greed. Instead, trial lawyers also create stories in their heads about what the plaintiff must have done to cause his own injuries.[5]

It may seem odd that trial lawyers are as quick as any focus-group respondent or juror to blame the plaintiff for his own injuries. But the tendency is unconscious, caused in part by defensive attribution. If you can explain away the plaintiff's misfortune by attributing fault to him, then you can defend yourself

---

[5] We use the male pronoun here because the trial lawyers at our lectures nearly always assume that the mythical drunken, roughhousing plaintiff who fell over the railing was a man.

against danger, because you would never make the same poor choices or stupid mistakes that the plaintiff did. Even you, the trial lawyer, can feel the need to blame the plaintiff so you can feel safe.[6]

This is why framing (our tenth commandment for defeating juror bias) is so important.[7] Blaming the plaintiff is a natural, almost reflexive behavior. Early jury research is the time to explore which of your facts will best redirect jurors' attention to the defendant's conduct that actually caused the harm.

All Five Biases at Work

An easy way to see all five biases at work is to analyze the obstacles in a medical negligence claim for a failure to diagnose cancer:

◆ As with any plaintiff's claim, jurors will be suspicious of the plaintiff's motives and the validity of the claim, especially when the claim is coming from a layperson against a respected member of the medical community.

◆ Cancer happens, and it is not always (or even usually) preventable. So stuff-happens jurors, as well as many others, don't understand why or how you can bring a lawsuit because the plaintiff has cancer.

◆ Jurors will think that suing a doctor because a person got cancer victimizes jurors and the community by raising medical and insurance costs, as well as driving doctors out of the jurisdiction or into retirement, thereby reducing access to health care.

◆ In cancer cases, defensive attribution often kicks in, driving jurors to find behaviors the plaintiff engaged in that put the plaintiff at risk: Did the plaintiff smoke? Did the plaintiff have

---

[6] *See* chapter 1, "Defensive Attribution," page 35.

[7] *See* "Build the Frame" in chapter 2, page 56.

an unhealthy diet? Did the plaintiff exercise regularly? Was the plaintiff careless when working around paints or chemicals?

◆ And, as you saw in the focus-group example of the woman whose breast cancer went undiagnosed, respondents blame the plaintiff for lacking personal responsibility by not following up or not knowing something was wrong, regardless of the medical advice the plaintiff received.

USING FOCUS GROUPS TO LEARN WHAT'S IMPORTANT TO JURORS

Not all land mines fall neatly into one of the five Jury Bias Model categories, of course. A case can just as easily blow up over misinformed preconceptions about your client's injuries, or a piece of information the jurors expected to hear but didn't. Good lawyers continually lament that they don't know what jurors want to hear. That's another reason for using concept focus groups. They'll tell you not only what jurors believe based on their life experiences, but also what they think is important.

Anything jurors think is important should be important to you. You will not shake them of their beliefs. We have learned that focus-group respondents will actually manufacture facts to justify their preconceptions about an issue. It happens all the time, in fact. To support a tenuous position given the facts as explained to the group, someone often makes up a fact and then claims: "That's what the lawyer told us." In reality, no one said anything like it. The psychological principle of belief perseverance leads jurors to cling to a belief once they've adopted it, even if it lacks a basis in fact. The answer to this challenge is to use jury research to learn what jurors think is important and then develop your trial story with that knowledge in mind.

Misconceptions about Injuries

In some types of cases, jurors have a lot of preconceptions and misconceptions about what your client's injuries should look like. This is often true in traumatic brain injury (TBI) and mild traumatic brain injury (MTBI) cases. These are beliefs you need to understand and prepare for in advance of trial.

In concept focus groups, we have asked what a brain-injured person looks like, and we've encountered many answers to the question, some surprising and others disturbing:

"They usually have a droopy mouth."

"They have one eye a little bit off."

"How long has he been brain injured? Because brain cells recreate themselves. I know that for a fact. When you lose brain cells, they grow back."

Without jury research, you might not discover that humans grow good-as-new gray matter the way lizards grow back a tail. Yet this is information you need so that you can deal with the facts jurors think are important, in addition to the facts you know are important. In concept focus groups, we also explore whether the way a traumatic brain injury occurred jibes with the jurors' preconceptions of how the injury could happen. Do the jurors understand that even a mild injury can cause extensive damage? Do they remember that the mild concussion Justin Morneau suffered in 2010 while sliding into second base actually sidelined a four-time All Star for half the season?

Because if the jurors understand that, then the facts you develop in your own trial story can support a similar understanding. In MTBI cases, we also use concept focus groups to learn whether jurors are likely to dispute whether the plaintiff's symptoms are in fact caused by a brain injury. Maybe the plaintiff is just goofy or ditzy or even making it up. Jury research will show you what jurors believe about injuries they can't see, hear, or touch. Whatever the jurors think or believe, it's important. Once you know, you can dig for the facts you need to develop your case core and trial story with the jurors' beliefs in mind.

Missing Information

Have you ever found yourself unable to focus on someone's conversation when he glosses right past something that's really important to you? Imagine, for example, trying to persuade a pro baseball general manager back in 2002 to study on-base percentages when all he could think about was recruiting a home-run slugger. Unless you were talking to the Oakland A's Billy Beane, you'd have been wasting your breath. Jurors get similarly hung up on their own preconceived ideas and beliefs.

Many years ago, Wenner and his law partner, Howard Snyder, had a case against the University of Arizona. They represented a young woman in her twenties who collapsed while exercising on a stationary bicycle in the university recreation center. The students working at the center failed to perform CPR, and the young woman suffered a brain injury. The lawsuit alleged that the student-employees should have been trained in CPR and that they should have performed it.

Six times Wenner and Snyder focus-grouped the case, and six times they were disappointed. They were not hopeful. Each time Cusimano and Wenner discussed it, Wenner kept telling Cusimano, "All the focus groups want to talk about is whether the young woman was turning blue." For focus-group members, if she was turning blue, she obviously wasn't getting enough oxygen and needed CPR. Turning blue was a heuristic they were using to make their own determination about whether the young woman needed CPR.

From a medical or legal viewpoint, the issue was unimportant because the standard of care at the time for administering CPR was unrelated to the question of whether a patient was turning blue. But to Cusimano, who was not deeply enmeshed in the case, the answer was clear-cut: "If the focus groups want to know whether she was turning blue, that's an important fact. If she was, put it in there." In the end, Wenner and Snyder won at trial, and their client received a very good verdict.

The case highlights two important points. First, use concept focus groups to discover any issue, whether arising from juror bias or from some other cause, which is likely to derail the jurors. And second, don't think for a moment that you possess the objectivity to conduct the focus group yourself. When you are too close to your own case, as was Wenner—even though he's an experienced trial lawyer, trial consultant, and someone who understands psychology—you sometimes can't see the stumbling blocks right in front of you.

USING A TRIAL CONSULTANT TO CONDUCT JURY RESEARCH

The following are several questions you may want to ask when you consider whether or not to use a trial consultant:

◆ What kind of services do you offer?
◆ Is your work research-based, experience-based, or both—and can you please explain why and how?
◆ Do you conduct concept focus groups?
◆ Can you provide references or past results?
◆ Do you work for both plaintiffs and defendants?
◆ Have you studied conscious and unconscious decision-making?
◆ What is your education and experience?
◆ How do you charge? Fee per service? Hourly? Contingency? (In most states, consultants must be lawyers in order to work on contingency, unless they have a contract with your client.) Combination? When do you expect payment?

Initially, you and your consultant should focus on determining which types of research tools make sense for the case. Some cases don't warrant the expense of one or more focus groups, and that's something you want to explore up front. For cases in which focus groups do make financial sense, the next issue is one of timing. Ideally, contact your consultant early enough to allow time to do concept focus groups while discovery is still in progress.

Concept focus groups help guide your discovery by revealing which facts you need to emphasize. The open discovery period will give you the opportunity to develop those specific facts. Even if you don't contact a consultant until after the discovery deadline, the consultant will make a difference for you. A consultant will provide the biggest benefit to you, however, if you have the chance, during discovery, to learn the necessary facts your focus groups establish you need, and not during (or after) trial.

Contacting a consultant early in your case provides other benefits as well. It gives them the opportunity to help you with long-term trial coaching by using the appropriate research tool at the appropriate time anywhere along the trial continuum. Depending on the size of the case and the time line, for instance, they might recommend a structured focus group or mini-mock trial later in the process to test your trial story or get a reading on your experts, on your exhibits, or on you. In fact, in the best of all possible worlds, you would contact a consultant even before you decide to accept what you know will be an expensive, major case.

For many of Winning Works' clients, we've begun a more holistic approach in working with them. We help lawyers analyze their inventory and highlight the cases with issues. Big cases are expensive cases. Before someone spends $200,000 or $300,000 to litigate a case and discover its weak spots, it often makes sense to spend a small fraction of that on jury research, early in the case, to learn how to fill in the gaps and make the case stronger.

If we learn, in our initial consultations, that the case justifies the expense of concept focus groups and that there is sufficient time to conduct them, what's next? Usually, our clients try to start off by sending us a file cabinet full of documents, which is made no less burdensome by virtue of its digital cabinetry. It reminds us of something Mark Twain reportedly wrote to a friend: "A successful book is not made of what is in it, but of what is left out of it."

There are several problems with sending your trial consultant too much information. First, it's more than they have time to read. Second, if they know too much about the case, they won't have the clear mind they need to conduct a proper concept focus group. And third, their acceptance of your entire file cabinet would only deprive you of the opportunity to sit down and really think about what's important in your own case.

It's understandable that many excellent lawyers, who have invested huge amounts of time and money into a case, have difficulty providing an elevator speech describing their case. Getting a case prepared for trial is difficult, and it's not easy reducing it to its essence.

In a complicated drug warning case, the answer to the question "What's your case about?" could be "This case is about whether a drug company that produces and sells a drug with a known risk to patients should share with the medical community all the necessary information doctors need to know about the drug to eliminate needless risk to the patient. In other words, share with the doctors and the medical community all the good and bad information—the risks, the benefits, and how to tell if the drug is helping or hurting—so the doctors have all the knowledge they need to properly treat and care for their patients."

When we start working with a lawyer, we ask that our client begin by simplifying the case. We ask that she give us a three-to -five-page neutral summary, one-or-two-page summaries of both the plaintiff's position and the defendant's position, and a list of the three to five critical issues in the case that reflect the strengths and weaknesses of all sides. We take the jury research from there. Our first step is to schedule a concept focus group, which could easily take a couple of weeks or longer to accomplish. Focus groups, like automobiles, vary greatly in cost, size, and quality. It depends on what you need and want.

Your consultants should collaborate with you to help decide what makes the most sense for a particular case and then handle all the logistics. They locate the facility for holding the focus group in the community where your case is filed. They handle the process of recruiting people to participate. And they take care of all the administrative aspects of the focus group. All you should have to do is provide your consultant with the case information and walk in the door at the appointed day and time.

At Winning Works, we usually meet with the client for a few hours the day before the focus group to make sure we are providing what is needed. After the focus group, we generally debrief with the trial team and follow with an oral or written report, or both, as requested. We then provide an analysis and make suggestions regarding further preparations.

Many readers doubtlessly plan to use what they learn in these pages to eliminate the middleman and conduct their own focus groups without hiring a trial consultant. We understand the temptation to cut costs. Three of us are longtime trial lawyers who appreciate firsthand the expense involved in managing significant personal injury litigation.

Conducting your own jury research is not easy to do, as Wenner learned in the case we discussed involving the young college student who needed CPR. As respondents in six focus groups kept asking, "Was she turning blue?" Wenner had difficulty seeing that the issue was of great importance to jurors because it wasn't something he, as the lawyer in the case, was focused on. He was too close to the case to step back and view it through the eyes of potential jurors. Lack of sufficient (or any) objectivity, then, is one reason not to play the role of trial consultant in your own case.

Conducting effective focus groups and other jury research requires considerable understanding of the social science of decision-making. As in any other field, the more experience you have, the better you become. Without experience in jury research or knowledge of the psychology and social science that supports the research, it can be easy to base your decisions on flawed intuition.

The Bottom Up approach to jury research and case preparation is an empirically based model. In the process we've developed, you don't investigate the facts at step one and stop. Or do a focus group at step two and then move to step three. To build your case effectively, you start by investigating the facts. Then, concept focus groups alert you to challenges in the case and tell you what additional facts you need to reframe the issues. Once you go back and flesh out those facts, you continue with jury research to ensure that you're developing a winning trial story. Our process for successful case preparation is based on repeated validation, not guesswork.

In addition to method, experience, and a science-based approach to jury research and case preparation, there's one more thing a good consultant can offer.

We enjoy helping lawyers help their clients. We know that being a trial lawyer is a huge responsibility—to your client, your office, and your family. We tell the truth, but we don't do it in a way that brutalizes the lawyer's ego. We laugh a lot in the midst of a serious endeavor—achieving justice for the client. But in addition to everything else we believe we bring, we also believe part of our job is to make the lawyer's job easier.

Why does this matter? Because working with a trial consultant on any sizable case should be a creative collaboration. It's not like hiring a brilliant orthopedic to fix your knee even though he's known to be a jerk. You're unconscious during surgery. But you're very much part of the action when it comes to developing a trial story and representing the rights of your client. It's important that you trust and create a rapport with your trial consultant because you're going to rely on one another to get the job done for the plaintiff.

WHAT WE HAVE LEARNED
Jury Research

Jury research is step two in the Bottom Up case preparation method and it is the most important part. Early jury research is critical to understanding jurors' beliefs and biases and to learning what they find important. When using concept focus groups early in your case, you may learn that your case is not at all about what you think it is. The critical fact for jurors may be something you considered unimportant. Find out what potential jurors think, and construct your case based on a story that's consistent with what they already believe.

Use focus groups as a guide for the facts you need to look for and develop during discovery. Validate the information you receive from focus groups with other research tools, such as the following:

- Peer research
- Media
- Similar lawsuits
- Online focus groups

- ◆ Surveys
- ◆ Instant feedback
- ◆ Mock trials

Then use what you've learned from early jury research to develop a case core and trial story that builds on the beliefs your jurors already have. It's difficult for lawyers to conduct their own jury research because they are often so invested in their cases that they can no longer be objective. As a result, when time and resources permit, trial consultants are better suited to conduct focus groups and other types of jury research.

6

BUILDING
THE CASE CORE

After you've investigated the facts and conducted your initial jury research with concept focus groups, the third step in Bottom Up case preparation is to develop the case core. The case core is the heart of your case—its underlying principle. Many lawyers refer to this as the theme, or as Cusimano likes to call it, "the moral essence" of your case. In our view, a case core has two parts: the first part is the moral of the case, and the second part is the simple story—a single sentence or short paragraph that describes what the case is about.

PART ONE: THE MORAL

The first part of your case core should be the case's moral. What is it about the injustice done to your client that's going to stick in the jury's craw? The moral of your case should be something that would be universally agreed on if you stated it. But it's not

113

like the moral of the story at the end of one of Aesop's fables. In fact, you may decide against ever expressly stating the moral of your case at trial. Develop your case's moral for yourself so you never lose sight of the underlying message you want to communicate through every piece of evidence you assemble, be it for trial, mediation, or settlement conference.

The following are a few examples we've seen lawyers successfully use as the moral of their case:

- ◆ At a minimum, care should equal risk.
- ◆ This car had every option but safety.
- ◆ This case is about closing the gap between what is and what should have been.
- ◆ A hospital is supposed to help, not hurt.
- ◆ This is a case about broken promises and broken dreams.
- ◆ A moment of carelessness caused a lifetime of misery.
- ◆ This case is about a lane change that caused a life change.
- ◆ With your help, we—laypeople—can fight city hall.

These are all morals or themes that we've heard lawyers successfully use at trial and while preparing their cases. Spend time investigating the facts and conducting jury research and the moral of your case should begin to emerge.

PART TWO: A SIMPLE STORY

The second part of the case core is the simple story of what your case is about. It might be a sentence or a very short paragraph—something along the lines of a tweet or elevator speech. The simple story should be easy enough to understand that a ten- to twelve-year-old child would easily grasp it. And it should move the listener to action.[1]

An example of a simple story comes from one of Cusimano's cases in which his elderly client went into the local hospital for an extensive physical examination. Because of her age, she was listed as a patient "at risk for fall." Protocol required that the hospital staff help her when going to the restroom. As health-care workers attempted to take her to the bathroom, someone stumbled and dropped her, breaking her back. The moral essence of the case: hospitals are supposed to help, not hurt. The simple story: Mrs. Ellison walked into the hospital for a physical examination, and three days later, she was rolled out with a broken back. Make them responsible (or in the alternative: make them pay).

In the breast cancer case we discussed earlier,[2] the simple story might be this: The plaintiff trusted her doctor, but his careless office procedures left her husband and three children without a wife or mother. Hold the doctor responsible.

CASE CORE POINTERS

As trial lawyers and consultants, we've tried a lot of different approaches for developing an effective case core. While there's no substitute for experience (good and bad), what follows is a discussion of some of the most important lessons we've learned.

---

[1] We first learned this concept from Katherine James, Alan Blumenfeld, and Joshua Karton when they worked together as trial consultants. They referred to it as a "telegram."

[2] *See* chapter 5, "Failure to Diagnose Breast Cancer," page 97.

THE CASE CORE IS YOUR COMPASS IN PREPARATION AND TRIAL

In Bottom Up case preparation, the primary purpose for developing an effective case core early on is to help you stay on message. It is the defense lawyer's job to ensure that you don't. All the defenses are there to water down your case and distract jurors from focusing on the defendant who is responsible for your client's injuries. Until you develop the core of your case, you don't really appreciate what your case is about. But once you know, the case core becomes your compass to remind you of where you are and where you're going.

As simple organizing principles, the moral of the case and the simple story never need to be stated at trial. Rely on them to keep you on course. Let them prevent you from chasing every rabbit the defense lets out of the cage. Remember the case Cusimano consulted on where the vacation chalet slid down the mountain after just one night's occupancy? It would have been distracting to deal with the suggestion that a tremor might have set the new house in motion. That speculation had nothing to do with the moral of the case or the simple story. Sticking to your case core will make it less likely that red herrings arise. For example, the simple story in that case was that "XYZ Construction Inc. installed the gas fireplace with low-cost, untested workers rather than qualified installers, causing an explosion and injuries. Hold them responsible."

Use your case core to ask yourself, "Does it strengthen my case to introduce a piece of evidence or call a particular witness?" If the answer is no, leave that rabbit alone. Don't dilute your message by cluttering up the record. One of the other common temptations we face as trial lawyers is to spend hours cross-examining the defendant's expert to undermine her credibility. What this does in reality is tell the jury that the witness's testimony is vitally important. Otherwise, you wouldn't expend so much time and energy attempting to discredit her.[3]

We file suit based on every possible legal theory: negligence, breach of contract, breach of warranty, product liability, conspiracy, and punitive damages. We attack our opponent's witnesses in lengthy, hyper-technical battles. But what carries the day is a simple story, plain and clear, with a moral underpinning with which no one would quarrel.

Understand the essence of your case. Knowing what your case is truly about will give you the confidence to keep yourself and the jury focused on *your* trial story, instead of the defendant's.

FOCUS GROUPS WILL GUIDE YOU TO THE CASE CORE

If you use concept focus groups as we recommend, they will lead you to your case's core. When you are busy analyzing your case the way you've been trained to do, it's easy to forget how the jury will see it. But if you listen to what focus-group participants tell you, the case core often jumps right out at you.

Turning back to the breast cancer case, Cusimano and Wenner conducted mock trials and structured focus groups in that case nine times and lost each time. They used some of the best trial lawyers in the country to present the plaintiff's case. Their exhibits were top dollar. But they lost nine times in a row.

The first nine times, the moral had been about money—about the doctor streamlining his practice to make money. Cusimano and Wenner didn't win any focus groups until they changed the moral of the case to this: the level of medical care should at least equal the medical risk. They highlighted all of the evidence that

---

[3] For more on this, *see* chapter 7, "Developing the Trial Story," page 127.

pointed to that conclusion. The required competent medical care was simple.

All the doctor had to do was call his patient and ask her to come to the office to discuss her test results. But he didn't even do that. On the other hand, the risk—death—was huge. Cusimano and Wenner didn't need fancy exhibits. The most effective exhibit they used was a simple board with the message "Care = Risk" written on it. The two things didn't match up and the next focus group saw that. To be sure of their analysis, Cusimano and Wenner tested it two more times and won again both times.

In the breast cancer case, the care should have equaled the risk, but it didn't. Who could disagree with that? If someone comes to the emergency room bleeding to death, should the care that patient receives not be greater than the attention given to a person who comes in with a sore knee? Of course it should. At a minimum, the care should equal the risk. How did we ultimately discover that winning case core?

We learned it from listening to focus groups.[4] We didn't win that case with a moral of "profits over people" even though it was true. The thing people related to most was the lack of a lock-tight system that would prevent the doctor's mistake from happening. And that's why concept focus groups are so valuable.

Going into a focus group, no one knows what's going to unlock the case for you. You have to suspend judgment until the focus groups show what's truly important. That's what happened in the breast cancer case. We finally paid attention to the focus-group participants who kept asking, "Why wasn't there some procedure in place for dealing with test results for patients who might have cancer? Cancer is a big deal!"

The focus groups led us straight to the case core that worked. It's important to pay attention to the participants' choice of words

---

[4] For an analysis of our focus groups involving the breast cancer case, *see* Neal Feigenson, *Legal Blame: How Jurors Think and Talk About Accidents* (Washington, DC: American Psychological Association, 2001).

and their body language. We listen carefully to their questions until we feel confident that we understand how they're putting the story together in their heads. Focus groups are the closest thing we have to a meaningful give-and-take with the jury. That's why we spend a lot of time following up on the participants' reactions, learning why they feel the way they do, how they relate one concept with another, and what they would need to hear to find for the plaintiff. When you understand all of that, you're well situated to find the case core that will work best for your client.

YOUR CLIENTS MAY SHOW YOU THE CORE OF YOUR CASE

As surprising as this sounds, many lawyers who are struggling to develop the core of their case don't think to start at an obvious spot—their client. It's a fundamental rule in medicine that if the doctor listens long enough to her patient, the patient will diagnose his own condition. But many doctors cut off their discussion with a patient after only a few seconds. Unfortunately, a lot of lawyers do the same thing. Yet the key to the core of your case may be sitting in the chair in front of your desk, just waiting for you to find it. The only way to find out is actually to listen to your client.

This is a lesson Cusimano learned many years ago in a case we previously discussed. He represented a woman who received compression fractures in her back after hospital staff members dropped her on the floor during what was supposed to be a routine visit for a physical. All along, Cusimano assumed the case would settle, but when the hospital made no offer, he really paid attention to his client in a way he should have, but hadn't before. Sitting in his office with a legal pad, Cusimano went through a list of perfunctory questions:

- How long did you stay in bed?
- Did you have to use a walker?
- Did you take pain medication?
- How many times did you see the doctor?

The woman began to cry. "Mrs. Ellison, have I said something to hurt your feelings?" Cusimano asked. Cusimano's client then told him her story.

Her husband died of cancer while her lawsuit was pending. Cusimano had known this and had sent her a note of condolence. But he knew nothing of their relationship. After her husband's chemotherapy treatments, she was in the habit of sitting in a chair next to his bed all night so that if he became nauseated, he would not aspirate on his own vomit.

The man loved biscuits and gravy. Every morning he was well enough to eat, Mrs. Ellison would fry up some bacon and serve it to her husband along with biscuits and gravy. But after her back injury, she explained she could no longer do those things for him in the waning weeks of his life. She couldn't sit up next to him. She couldn't help him move in the bed when he needed to. She couldn't even fix him breakfast. Cusimano had been thinking he had a case about an elderly woman with some uncomfortable compression fractures when the entire time he had a tragic love story.

Fortunately for Mrs. Ellison, Cusimano did learn what the case was about before trial and was able to help the jury see it too, which resulted in a handsome verdict for her. But the case would have turned out differently had Cusimano not taken the time to really listen to his client.

AVOID BUILDING YOUR CASE AROUND MONEY

There was a time when a trial lawyer might persuasively tell the jury that the case was about the Golden Rule and not the Rule of Gold. In today's world of tort reform, that is not a moral of the case that you can state out loud. The same is probably true if the moral of your case is about a company willing to sacrifice people in pursuit of profits. In the "olden days," you could stand up and say that a negligent corporation had just been too greedy. But in focus groups now, we see people's eyes begin to roll.

Jurors today see the greediest person in the courtroom as you: "Lawsuit Lottery." "Jackpot Justice." These two-word jingles have transformed even innocuous-sounding words such as "win" or "award" into off-color language to be avoided in the courtroom.

An award of medical damages is the same as the Publisher's Clearing House Award, right? Winning a verdict in a dram shop case is just like winning at the slots in Vegas as far as jurors are concerned. We have to distinguish ourselves from the kind of lawyers that tort reformers incessantly decry.

None of this means that you shouldn't focus on the defendant's choice to put profits over people, or even make that your theme. It's just risky to tell the jury that it's the moral of your case. You have to show them instead. But this is something you should be doing anyway. It's always more effective to allow the jurors to reach a conclusion on their own than to announce in advance what they should think or do.

If the moral of your case is that the defendant chose to sacrifice people for profits, establish a framework for allowing jurors to make that determination themselves. How did the defendant act in a self-interested manner, bestowing a benefit to himself or his practice or his corporation to the plaintiff's detriment? Don't say it—show it.

Take the breast cancer case as an example. The plaintiff's doctor established a system in his office that depended on two physician extenders: a nurse practitioner and a physician's assistant. The system allowed the doctor to treat more patients than he could have done by himself. Jurors don't need to be told that the doctor's motivation in seeing more patients was to bring in more money. They can reach that conclusion on their own.

There's nothing wrong with a doctor hiring nurse practitioners or physician's assistants so he can see a hundred as opposed to forty patients a day. And there's nothing wrong with making more money. Still, when it comes to informing patients about the results of critical tests like a mammogram used to screen for cancer, it is wrong to delegate that task without safeguards—especially when the results are ambiguous.

The key to using profits over people as the moral of the case in that scenario is in showing, not telling, the jury that the doctor was more interested in building his practice than in building relationships with his patients. That stains the defendant's character. The jury will see that if the doctor had been focused on his patient's well-being when the mammogram results came back, he would have explained the results to her himself and ensured the necessary further testing. The moral of the case will be obvious.

A SYSTEM FAILURE MAKES A BETTER CASE CORE THAN A SINGLE INCIDENT

When possible, find a moral that applies to an entire system as opposed to a particular incident. Show the jurors how an entire system was broken and it will dramatically influence the way they view your case.

Sticking with the breast cancer case as our example, one of the doctor's defenses in the case was to blame the plaintiff. The onus was on the patient, the doctor protested, to schedule an appointment to see the doctor even after the doctor's staff had told her there was no problem with her mammogram results and she should come back in a year. We turned that around and put the responsibility where it belonged: with the doctor who should have created an office procedure that would have prevented patients with ambiguous results on cancer screening tests from falling through the cracks.

A system-failure approach is powerful in part because it helps blunt the effect of the defensive-attribution bias. The breast cancer case is the one in which we first saw the defensive-attribution bias at work. Women in the age bracket most susceptible to breast cancer had the harshest attitude toward the plaintiff. At the time, this was completely counterintuitive for us. But we learned that they were afraid. If one woman could die of breast cancer because of her doctor's careless mistake, then these women in our focus groups were at risk for the same fate.

To remove the risk in their minds, these women set up a psychological defense mechanism by blaming the plaintiff instead of the doctor. If they had been in the plaintiff's shoes, they imagined that they would have prevented the harm by demanding that the doctor order additional tests or by seeking a second opinion. By developing a case core that focused on the breakdown of a system in the doctor's office, we shifted the respondents' attention away from the plaintiff and back to the doctor who could have saved the plaintiff's life. All the doctor had to do was institute and adhere to a system that prevented patients with cancer from falling through the cracks—to make the care equal to the risk.

Sometimes your case may involve a broken system and you don't even realize the importance of it until a focus group points it out. A few years ago, a client of ours represented the family of a nineteen-year-old woman who went into the emergency room for treatment and died fifteen hours later. Two different doctors at two different points in her care made a differential diagnosis that included the condition with which she presented. Yet no one ever ordered the test needed to rule out the differential diagnosis. Instead, hospital staff administered fluids, which was actually the worst thing you could do for someone with her condition. Over the hours, she grew progressively worse until she died.

When we started consulting with our client on a trial strategy, we wanted to be sure that we told the story so that jurors would understand the medicine. But our focus groups told us that it wasn't about the medicine. What really irritated the focus groups was the six hours the young woman spent sitting in the hallway waiting to be moved from the ER to the pediatric ward. We then learned from our client—the lawyer who represented the young woman's family—that the hospital had been reprimanded earlier for its failure to maintain a proper boarding policy.

That was the case core right there. The young woman never received proper treatment because the hospital never put in place a proper boarding procedure to prevent critically ill patients from languishing for hours without treatment in the hallway. Once we developed the case core around the hospital's decision not to develop or adhere to proper boarding procedures, our client was able to obtain a favorable settlement from the hospital.

This case illustrates two important issues involving focus groups. The first is one we have already discussed in this chapter: allow your focus groups to lead you to an effective case core that will resonate with your jury. And the second: get the facts and never leave them.[5] In this case, when we learned what was most troubling for ordinary people—the young woman was forced to wait hours in the hospital hallway—our client immediately referred us to discovery he'd done earlier about the hospital's previous reprimand. With that information, we were able to frame and reframe the story.

---

[5] *See* chapter 4, "Investigating the Facts," page 71.

If he had not already discovered that information, however, it would have been time for him to go back to the facts and do the necessary discovery to assemble all the facts related to the young woman's long wait in the hallway. Did that wait violate hospital protocols? Were there procedures in place? What were the boarding policies in other hospitals? Focus groups often teach us that facts that may seem unimportant at first turn out to be the puzzle pieces that form the central core of our case.

THE BEST CASE CORE MAKES THE BEST USE OF FACTS

As trial consultants, our job is to help lawyers structure their cases so the jurors focus on the good facts and underweight the bad facts. That's what an effective case core will do—focus jurors' attention on your best facts and distract them from facts that aren't as helpful.

In the breast cancer case example, a case core that focused on the doctor's choice not to adhere to a reliable procedure for informing potential cancer patients of their test results was persuasive. The system-failure approach diverted attention from what some jurors perceived as an isolated occurrence in which a single patient was herself careless in not following up with her doctor more aggressively.

If your case involves a big rig collision on a foggy day, the case core might not focus on the wreck itself. Instead, the moral of the case may be found in the hours or weeks leading up to the crash in which a driver with sleep apnea struggled to meet his employer's new on-time delivery quotas.

In the Mega Mart case, the simple story that was effective with jurors concerned the retailer's lackluster efforts to make the store safe for shoppers on a rainy day when it knew floors would be slick. The local store didn't bother to follow the national retailer's written policies. In addition, the store's merchandising displays intentionally drew customers' attention away from dangers on the wet floor. Relying on a case core to structure the case in this way changes the essence of the case from one about a scatterbrained woman who slips on a rain puddle to a case about a store that didn't take the time to follow its own procedures to ensure shoppers' safety.

In each of these examples, the case facts remain the same. But an effective case core will help you frame and reframe your case so that jurors overweight the helpful facts and underweight those that may be troublesome.

WHAT WE HAVE LEARNED

Build the Case Core

A thoughtfully developed case core is an important tool that helps prepare and structure a case for trial, mediation, arbitration, and settlement. A case core has two parts: the moral of the case and a simple story no longer than a sentence or short paragraph. As you develop your case core, keep these pointers in mind:

- The case core is your compass in case preparation and trial.
- Focus groups will guide you to the case core.
- Your clients may show you the core of your case.
- Avoid just building your case around money.
- A system failure makes a better case core than a single incident.
- The best case core makes the best use of facts.

7

DEVELOPING THE
TRIAL STORY

Stories are magic. They grab jurors' attention, hold it, and blaze a trail for them to follow throughout trial. Along the way, jurors experience sights, sounds, thoughts, and emotions through the lens that you—the storyteller—provide. Stories significantly affect the way jurors think, how well they remember important facts, and the way they make decisions at the end of trial. Researchers tell us that there are three stages to the story model of jury reasoning.[1]

In the first stage, jurors evaluate the evidence to determine what happened. They formulate their own stories to use later in decision-making. Their information, of course, comes from the evidence the lawyers present at trial. But that evidence is

---

[1] Shelly Spiecker and Debra L. Worthington, "The Story Model of Juror Reasoning; A Mini Review," *Court Call*, The American Society of Trial Consultants (Summer 2002); *See also,* N. Pennington and R. Hastie, "The Story Model for Juror Decision Making" in, ed., R. Hastie, *Inside the Juror: The Psychology of Juror Decision Making* (New York: Cambridge University Press, 1993), 192–221.

then filtered through the jurors' own backgrounds, experiences, beliefs, and expectations. They rank the evidence they unconsciously deem as most important at the highest level. The stories jurors remember are the ones they create.

In the second stage, the jurors process the evidence in light of what they understand the legal verdict options will be. They may also mix in their own ideas about what happened.[2] Jurors search for an appropriate verdict based on the judge's instructions.

In the third stage, jurors try to match the stories they've created to a particular verdict class. If the story line fits a given category, they choose it; if not, they search for another one. Jurors' stories often represent relationships between the evidence, the jurors' memory of the evidence, and narrative constructs of the jurors' own schemas or thought patterns for organizing information.

Jurors enter the courtroom with their heads already filled with stories about you and your clients. Unfortunately, many of those stories are of the jackpot-justice and lawsuit-lottery variety, fueled by fifty years of misinformation from tort reform advocates. But even without the smear campaign, jurors would still be forming stories in their heads. We all do it. Sit in an airport for just one minute without looking at your phone, and you'll probably create half a dozen stories about the complete strangers walking by.

When you think about developing the trial story, consider the story of a little boy who watched a sculptor chisel away at a big block of granite. Over time, a magnificent lion emerged. The little boy said to the sculptor, "I got a question for you."

"Go ahead," replied the sculptor.

The boy asked, "How did you know that lion was in that rock?"

Instead of granite, your building materials are the facts you've already investigated—the strengths of the plaintiff's story, the

---

[2] N. Pennington and R. Hastie, "The Story Model for Juror Decision Making" in, ed., R. Hastie, *Inside the Juror: The Psychology of Juror Decision Making* (New York: Cambridge University Press, 1993), 192–221.

strengths of the defendant's story, the potential land mines, and the major concerns about liability, damages, or a particular witness. You should also make use of your jury research—the preordained patterns in the jurors' heads that will influence their view of the facts. Then apply the tools of Bottom Up case preparation to help your jury see the lion.

The first commandment of the Jury Bias Model is to develop an effective trial story. *The other nine principles really just explain what to include in a trial story to make it work.* In this chapter, we discuss how to develop an effective trial story. We refer to the commandments as they are used and explain how and why to rely on them for the greatest result.

FOCUS ON THE DEFENDANT

Begin your trial story with the defendant. As we've discussed before, you need to make the story about the defendant's wrongdoing, not the plaintiff's injuries. We know from our research that juries assign great importance to the plaintiff's conduct for a variety of reasons—evolutionary reasons, psychological reasons, and tort reform reasons. When jurors focus on the plaintiff, they fall back on one of the previously discussed five common juror biases: blame the plaintiff.[3]

Focusing on the defendant makes good use of the availability bias, and it is our fourth commandment for overcoming built-in jury biases.[4] If the centerpiece of your trial story is the plaintiff, the jurors will focus on the plaintiff. When that happens, jurors first think of changes in the plaintiff's conduct that would have

---

[3] *See* chapter 1, "The Jury Bias Model Part One," page 32.

[4] *See* a discussion of the availability bias in chapter 2, "The Jury Bias Model Part Two," page 49.

prevented the harm, and then, research shows, jurors proceed to blame the plaintiff.

But the availability bias teaches us that when you focus on the defendant, jurors engage in the same kind of thought exercise when considering the defendant's conduct. And they will be far more likely to blame the defendant.

Focusing on the defendant is also a good way to minimize the harmful impact of the plaintiff's conduct, insofar as it departs from the jurors' perceived ideal. If the jurors are consumed with the defendant's wrongdoing, they will be distracted from delving into the plaintiff's.

For many of our clients, beginning the trial story with the defendant rather than the plaintiff is counterintuitive. Some of our clients begin their trial story by saying something like, "This is the story of a healthy young man with a good job, a wife, and three small children at home." But when you start out that way, the jury doesn't know where the problem started. The problem didn't start with the plaintiff. It began with the defendant and the defendant's choices, actions, and inactions.

BEGIN THE STORY WITH THE DEFENDANT'S FIRST CHOICE THAT LED TO YOUR CLIENT'S HARM

Begin the trial story long before the events that occurred at the moment of the plaintiff's injuries. In a design defect case, the story might begin ten years before the date of the plaintiff's car crash—at the time the automobile manufacturer made the choice to incorporate a faulty ignition switch in the vehicle. The further back, the better. The manufacturer's choice to cut costs started the clock on a time line that would inevitably lead to something bad. The defendant might not have known when it would happen or who would be hurt, but now we know.

This is all part of the concept we discussed earlier about the trial story's arc.[5] When looking at what you need for legal proof, it's easy to restrict your thinking about liability to present-day events. You're also likely to view injuries strictly in terms of the plaintiff—her physical, emotional, and financial condition between the incident and the time of trial.

But when you broaden your scope to include jury proof, it's clear that the arc stretches further in both directions. Long before the injury, the defendant's conduct ensured that someone would be hurt at a future date. And the injuries don't stop with the plaintiff. When you emphasize jury proof, the jurors will think beyond your client to the broader implications for their own safety and the safety of their community. That's why a time line can be an effective trial exhibit to illustrate the trial story; at a glance, jurors can see where the trouble began—and that's always with the defendant sometime in the past.

Find Facts that Explain the Defendant's Conduct by Revealing the Stain on His Character

Remember, *stay within the facts*. You are not creating a granite lion; you are finding the lion within the granite. Look at the defendant's actions, choices, and decisions—all of it. Then meas ure those facts against what you've learned from focus groups about jurors' expectations of how the defendant should have behaved under the circumstances. An example of this is the pet-store manager's behavior in the slip and fall case, when he wouldn't let the injured woman use the store phone or let her sit in the front where she'd be visible.

---

[5] For a discussion of legal proof and jury proof, *see* chapter 4, "Investigating the Facts," page 72.

Revealing the stain on the defendant's character uses the fundamental attribution error—the focus of our sixth commandment—to your benefit.[6] People tend to attribute a person's choices and conduct to her personality rather than the situation in which she finds herself. This heuristic works against us with regard to the plaintiff; jurors tend to blame the plaintiff for her own injuries even when the defendant's misconduct is clear.

One challenge for trial lawyers is to show the jury that the injured plaintiff behaved as she did because of external circumstances beyond her control, not because of internal shortcomings. The opposite is true for defendants, however. The heuristic can work to our advantage concerning the defendant, especially when he has a character flaw or a hidden motive that in the jurors' minds explains his negligent conduct.

Sift through the facts until you uncover a character stain, and jurors will attribute the defendant's conduct to that shortcoming rather than view the wrongdoing as a simple mistake or reaction to external circumstances. Jurors want to understand why the defendant made the choices he did. Did a company act out of self-interest just to make a bigger profit? Was a defendant doctor in a hurry to make a tee time? Was a tired radiologist rushing to get home at the end of the day? Those are straightforward and credible explanations of the defendant's conduct that work to the plaintiff's advantage in the jurors' minds. You don't need a medical degree to understand that if a doctor is in a hurry, he is more likely to hurt someone than if he is acting with diligence, patience, and respect for his patients with life-threatening illnesses.

---

[6] For a discussion of the fundamental attribution error as it relates to the blame-the-plaintiff bias, *see* chapter 1, "The Jury Bias Model Part One," page 37.

Show, Don't Tell

Jurors do not want to be told what to do. For many trial lawyers, this concept is counterintuitive. Many trial lawyers have begun their opening statements this way: "This is a case about a negligent doctor in a hurry who caused the death of an innocent four-year-old child." But that statement is a judgment and a conclusion in itself.

Jurors react in knee-jerk fashion, thinking, "How do I know that's true? Why should I believe her?" In mock trials and focus groups, we've actually witnessed jurors who react by crossing their arms and looking at our trial lawyer clients with an expression that says, "Oh yeah?"

Bossart learned this lesson the hard way. In one of his own cases, during closing argument, he told a jury in Bismarck, North Dakota, that "to bring in a verdict for the defendant, you'd have to disbelieve every single witness the plaintiff called." Still, the jury had the power to do just that. As the trial court instructed, the jurors didn't have to believe a single one of the plaintiff's experts. And they didn't. It turned out that they were uninterested in having Bossart tell them what to do and think.

Nothing can save us from the fact that the life lessons we remember best are the ones we learn for ourselves. The same is true for jurors. Don't tell them; show them. Let them come to a conclusion on their own, and they will remember it when they file into the jury room to deliberate at the end of trial.

In the breast cancer case, the doctor was in a hurry. He was more focused on building his medical practice than in building relationships with his patients. He didn't follow up to notify his patient of the need for further testing, but he remembered to have his office call her for the next annual mammogram. That was the frame for the defendant's conduct.

But don't make an announcement of it. Instead, show the jurors so they come to that conclusion on their own.

A few years earlier, the cancer victim's doctor changed his office procedures after attending a seminar in Las Vegas that taught how to streamline his medical practice. He hired a nurse practitioner and a physician's assistant, which allowed him to take on many new patients. He used to see just forty patients in a day, and with the additional help, he could see a hundred. Before increasing his patient load so dramatically, the doctor had always spoken personally with patients about the results of mammograms and other critical tests or biopsies. But under the new structure, there wasn't time for that. The doctor had to delegate some of that work to the physician's assistant or nurse practitioner. Although some of the doctor's older patients commented on the change in procedures, the newer patients rarely grumbled about it.

The jury might hear these facts from the defendant doctor, or perhaps from the doctor's nurse who had worked in the office both before and after the staff additions. Either way, the jury will get the picture that the new office arrangement was for the doctor's benefit, not for his patients'. If the doctor had been interested in his patient's well-being, he would have personally discussed the mammogram results with her and ordered the necessary further tests.

In closing argument, you might suggest to the jurors in a quiet way that they probably had realized themselves after hearing the testimony of the doctor and his nurse that a doctor should treat only the number of patients that he can safely care for. You are just circling back around to the theme that you've seeded all along with your cross-examination of the doctor and his nurse as well as other evidence. And so, in closing, you can gently suggest the character stain you have established throughout the trial—that the defendant is a doctor who cares more about his pocketbook than his patients. This just affirms a conclusion the jurors likely reached on their own. It is always far more powerful to show jurors than to tell them.

INCLUDE JURY PROOF

Jury proof is another effective tool for developing a trial story.[7] The best trial story is sometimes one that is completely counter-intuitive. This is because many lawyers, who are so steeped in the law, naturally overlook the importance of jury proof.

Cusimano once consulted on a case in which a newborn suffered terrible injuries during a delivery by cesarean section. Initially, we worked to demonstrate that the hospital and the doctor had made poor choices and failed to operate in a timely manner. But we knew that the issue of medical liability—what the doctor should or shouldn't have done—was close. The issue was not going our way in focus groups, so we asked, "What would make you think differently about the case?" The response: "If there was something they could have done to get the mother into surgery more quickly, or if there was some kind of delay, we might feel differently."

So Cusimano went back to the facts to see what he might be missing. *Remember: never leave the facts.* The plaintiff's lawyers had not told him that when the hospital moved the mother to the delivery room, the door was locked. The nurses couldn't find the key. After their banging on the door, someone finally let them in. The delay was three minutes.

When a new focus group learned about the three-minute delay during which the nurses were locked out of the operating room, they concluded that the hospital was poorly run. They assumed that the incident was typical for the hospital involved. Proof of the three-minute delay gave the jurors what they needed to impose liability in a close case. Jury proof, not legal proof, won the case. Make jury proof part of every trial story.

---

[7] *See* our earlier discussion on legal proof versus jury proof in chapter 4, "Investigating the Facts," page 72.

You can find jury proof anywhere, of course. But you will often find facts for jury proof in the relationships between and among the people in your case. Think about the pet-store case we described earlier and the relationship between the pregnant woman who slipped and the store manager who would not allow her to use the phone to call her husband.[8] That relationship defined the defendant in the jurors' minds. Also consider the plaintiff's relationship with her family, her coworkers, her company, her clubs, her church, and her friends.

These relationships reveal to the jury what kind of person someone is. Is the plaintiff someone to be suspicious of, or does she remind the jurors of their next-door neighbor, who also delivers Meals on Wheels to homebound seniors? Creating empathy is our eighth commandment in overcoming common juror biases. Relationships are fertile grounds for facts to help jurors develop empathy for your client.

REFRAME FACTS

To develop an effective trial story, reframe the facts to direct the jury's focus. What do we mean by framing?

A monk says to the abbot, "May I smoke when I pray?"

A different monk asks, "May I pray when I smoke?"[9]

The action is the same in both questions. But our perceptions and judgments about one monk are starkly different from the other. That's because of framing. Remember that different presentations of the same issues or facts influence jurors' choices and judgments.

---

[8] *See* chapter 4, "Investigating the Facts," page 73.

[9] *See* Paul Brest and Linda Hamilton Krieger, *Problem Solving, Decision Making, and Professional Judgment: a Guide for Lawyers and Policymakers* (New York: Oxford University Press, 2010), 35.

The use of proper framing is critical to developing an effective trial story, and it is the topic of our tenth commandment for overcoming common juror biases. In a broad sense, outside the confines of psychology, the concept of framing refers to a way of structuring the trial story that allows jurors to review the facts through one filter as opposed to another. It is no secret that the way jurors view the facts will determine their decision.

Sometimes, however, effective framing can seem counterintuitive for many trial lawyers, but it's congruent with the way regular humans are hardwired. This is often true for trial stories in medical negligence cases that involve the interplay of three strong psychological principles: the need to live in a safe world, loss aversion, and adherence to the status quo. A winning trial story must address and harmonize these three elements:

1. Need for a safe world: Jurors, like all of us, need to believe that they live in a safe world. Our hospitals, doctors, and products must all be safe. If we didn't believe this at some level, we'd be walking around scared to death all day and accomplish nothing.

2. Loss aversion: People are loss averse. We are two times more motivated to avoid a loss than to achieve a gain.[10] We don't want to relinquish something we already own, even after the thing has lost its value—like shares of stock or ski pants that fit twenty years ago.

3. Status quo: We are also held captive by the status quo bias. People are reluctant to change. In your law office, nobody wanted to switch from WordPerfect to Word, or from Westlaw to Lexis, and especially not from Coke to Pepsi. Jurors also are inclined to maintain the status quo. That can work against you because the defendant has the money and the plaintiff needs it. Your job is to influence the jury to take the money

---

[10] Amos Tversky and Daniel Kahneman, "Advances in Prospect Theory: Cumulative Representation of Uncertainty," *Journal of Risk and Uncertainty* 5 (1992): 297–323.

from the defendant and give it to the plaintiff—to disrupt the status quo between the defendant and the plaintiff.

Most trial lawyers have never considered the combined effect of these three principles when developing a trial story. But this is at the core of what we do as trial consultants using the Bottom Up case preparation process. If you frame the trial story to persuade jurors that something they themselves rely on is dangerous and should be made safer, you ask them to reject three of the stories already playing in their heads: that the world is safe, that they don't want to lose that safety by admitting that it doesn't exist, and that change is unnecessary.

For example, you will rarely convince jurors in a smaller community that their hospital is unsafe. The mother of three children whose family relies on the local doctors for medical care is not going to relinquish her belief in the town hospital or budge from the status quo. So, what we must do is develop a trial story that is consistent with what the jurors already believe. This is the purpose of our second commandment, which is to develop a trial story that accounts for the confirmation bias—the tendency of jurors to listen for and retain information that confirms what they already believe.

How do we do it? Reframe the trial story to account for loss aversion. Show jurors that a decision for the plaintiff is a choice not to relinquish the level of safety the community already possesses. It's a decision to hold the line on safety.

In a medical negligence case, many lawyers craft a story about a dangerous hospital with lax safety measures. But this is inconsistent with what the jurors already believe or want to believe. Emphasize instead how great the hospital is, and its high safety standards. Instead of comparing a defendant hospital to other, safer hospitals, contrast the hospital's actual substandard performance with its customary excellence. What happened is that someone failed to live up to the hospital's high standards.

A decision for the plaintiff prevents the loss of existing safety standards by restoring and reinforcing them. A decision for the defendant changes the status quo by relaxing safety standards in the future and risking similar injuries for others. The plaintiff seeks to hold the line on safety. The defendant wants to lower the bar.

In the Mega Mart slip and fall example we discussed earlier, it would be tempting to frame the big-box retailer as a heartless behemoth with no concern for its customers' safety.[11] But jurors are never going to embrace a trial story that would frighten them away from shopping at Walmart, Costco, or Target. So, our trial story focused on the store's attention to safety. On the day the plaintiff fell, the retailer showed a training video to its employees concerning safety protocols for rainy days. The Mega Mart where the jurors shop with their families is a safe place. But in the plaintiff's case, the manager and employees ignored the retailer's safety standards and chose to subject customers to a dangerous condition. A decision for the plaintiff affirms the Mega Mart's safety procedures and maintains the status quo. A decision for the defendant means a loss of those safety standards at the Mega Mart and possible injuries for future customers' families.

Don't frame the jurors' community as an unsafe world. Frame the defendant's conduct as a threat to the safety net that already exists. Hold the line on safety.

---

[11] *See* chapter 4, "Investigating the Facts," page 83.

ESTABLISH CREDIBILITY

Do not forget that the jury is suspicious of you, your client, and your client's case.[12] Use every opportunity to demonstrate the plaintiff's integrity, credibility, and willingness to accept personal responsibility in his own life. This is another way to develop empathy for the plaintiff, the eighth commandment of the Jury Bias Model,[13] and combat two of the five common juror biases—suspicion and personal responsibility.

A focus group always wants to know how many lawsuits the plaintiff has filed in the past. In almost every single one of our cases, of course, this is the only lawsuit the plaintiff has ever been involved in. Cusimano likes to say when questioning his client, "Mr. Jones, you look a little nervous, but try to relax. The jury is just here to find out the truth." More often than not, the plaintiff will answer: "Well, I've never been in a courtroom before. I've never done this before."

Always look for ways to address jurors' similar unasked questions, such as, "When did the plaintiff first see the doctor?" Or, "When did the plaintiff first see a lawyer?" Voir dire provides a simple way to address the personal-responsibility bias. For example, Cusimano often asks questions like the following:

- "Ms. Jones, would you stand up? Has anybody in the courtroom ever met Ms. Joyce Jones?" No.
- "From 1991 to 1996, Joyce went to Jacksonville University at night to earn her college degree. Did anybody here go to Jacksonville University during that time?" No.

---

[12] *See* the discussion of suspicion in chapter 1, "The Jury Bias Model Part One," page 22.

[13] *See* chapter 2, "The Jury Bias Model Part Two," page 55.

◆ "During the same time, Joyce worked at the Red Lobster four nights a week and delivered papers every morning. Have any of you worked for Red Lobster or the *Gadsden Times*?" No.

The Bottom Up case preparation process forces us to be creative and dig out all the facts. If your client worked as a babysitter when she was twelve or hoed sugar beets in the searing summer sun during high school, those are facts you can use to show the jury that your client has been a hardworking member of her community since the time she was a child. Time and again, we've heard focus groups saying, "I just don't believe that's the kind of person who would file a frivolous lawsuit and pretend to have a bad back. She doesn't seem to be that kind of person."

Remember that the suspicion bias works as much against you as it does your client. Look for ways to establish your own credibility with the jury. You might, for example, allow the jury to know in voir dire that, in contrast to the defendant's lawyers, you are part of the local community: "Ladies and gentlemen, let me reintroduce myself. My name is Sally Smithson and my partner, Opie Turner, and I have a two-person firm here in Peoria. You've already been introduced to the three defense attorneys from Hockum, Shockum & Sockum in Chicago. Is there anyone who would hold it against my client that he has just one lawyer, while the defendant has three?"

During trial, don't overlook further opportunities to prove your integrity. If, for example, you are cross-examining the defendant's witness and he unwittingly misspeaks and says something that actually helps your client, stop him right there: "Excuse me, did you realize you said such-and-such? Is that really what you meant?" The witness usually will reply, "Oh no, did I say that?" This small step will win you a great deal of credibility with the jury, and it won't cost you a thing. If you had tried to use the witness's misstatement against the defendant, the jury would've recognized it as a cheap shot anyway. By treating your opponent's witnesses fairly, you establish yourself as someone the jury can trust.

Remember, there's a difference between credibility and *truth*. You won't be able to persuade jurors of the truth if they don't believe it already. Recall the second commandment in the Jury Bias Model.[14] If, for example, you try to convince the jury panel in voir dire that the now notorious hot coffee case against McDonald's was not frivolous, you will lose all credibility with your potential jurors. They believe to their core that the case was indeed frivolous, even though it wasn't. Once people have already formed an opinion, you will be unable to persuade them that anything different is true. You can only strive to prove your own credibility so the jurors feel safe in trusting you to help them reach the right decision.

LESS IS BETTER

Do not force the jury to resolve too many issues. Spend time only on the issues you need resolved. Less is not more, but sometimes less is better. This is why: As their reward for listening to your trial story day after day in court, jurors expect to reach a resolution and achieve satisfaction in the end. If you overload the story with too many issues, jurors will only become confused, bogged down, and frustrated that they were unable to keep all the information you threw their way straight. You do not want anxious and cranky jurors deliberating over your case. Jurors prefer a problem they can solve; don't make it hard on them.

Give conscious thought throughout the case to the facts that don't belong in the story. During trial, this is a good rule of thumb: If what you are about to say will reinforce the case core, then proceed. If not, forget about it. In the breast cancer case we described earlier, would it matter if the defendant doctor played

---

[14] *See* chapter 2, "The Jury Bias Model Part Two," page 42.

golf at a municipal course every Saturday morning? Probably not. But could it help reveal a character stain if he left the office early on the day the plaintiff's mammogram results came in so he could fit in half a round at Mt. Paymore, the priciest country club in town? Yes, indeed.

The need to limit issues commonly arises as a matter of strategy on cross-examination, such as when the defendant brings in a qualified, credible expert. The temptation is to spend hours in cross-examination and try to assault the witness's credibility. But what you're really doing is signaling to the jury that this expert is really, really important.

You want to send the opposite message. Try to extract one or two quick concessions from the witness that reinforce your trial story; and if you don't need more, sit down. In one of Cusimano's cases, the trial judge allowed the defendants to call an unexpected expert at the last minute. The trial was in a small Alabama town and the expert lived in Seattle. According to the expert, he testified on direct that he traveled that distance because when he heard the case was being tried, he wanted to make sure that the truth came out. After a day and a half on direct, Cusimano's cross-examination consisted of two questions:

Q: Now let's see if I understand. You came all the way from Seattle, Washington, to Gadsden, Alabama, because you wanted to make sure that the truth came out. You're that kind of guy?

A: Yes.

Q: Did they pay you?

A: Yes.

Q: I don't have any other questions.

And that was it. The jurors saw that Cusimano was unperturbed by the testimony, and they disregarded it. Stick with your own trial story. Don't chase rabbits. Limit the issues the jury must consider.

MAKE IT UNDERSTANDABLE
AND INTERESTING

Comprehension is the *sine qua non* for communication. Make certain your trial story is understandable. It's difficult to overstate the importance of this rule. We have discovered, for example, that one of the reasons jurors focus on the plaintiff's conduct rather than the defendant's is that it is almost always easier to understand. That's because the plaintiff is a person and jurors generally understand what people should and should not do. Jurors don't know what a doctor or an engineer or a product manufacturer should do. It's easier to focus on the plaintiff's conduct because jurors understand it.

As a result, your trial story should describe the defendant's conduct in a way that makes it as easy to understand as running a red light. The trial story must educate the jurors to understand what was wrong and why. One of the difficulties in a complicated medical negligence or product liability case is that most lawyers have become accustomed to relying on experts to explain the defendant's conduct. Once the lawyer becomes proficient in the science or technology, she and the expert have a conversation at trial that explains in perfect detail exactly how the defendant failed to meet the applicable standard of care. The problem is that the jury doesn't understand a word of it.

The best remedy is to tell the trial story in simple language that every juror will understand. To make certain that jurors understand your presentation, pay attention to their faces and body language for signs of puzzlement or distress. When in doubt, ask a follow-up question or request that the witness repeat his answer. Don't move on from an important point until you are sure the jury has heard and understood that portion of your trial story.

Ideally, the trial story should be understandable and interesting for jurors. In the technical, sterile environment of the courtroom, sparkling conversation is difficult. Still, there is no better way to define your client, the defendant, or a witness than through examination and cross-examination. Skip legalese. It's neither understandable nor interesting.

To make the presentation of your trial story compelling, don't sanitize or homogenize your clients and witnesses. Though everyone has a unique way of speaking in everyday life, witnesses' speech patterns often become forced and flat when they take the stand. Encourage your clients and witnesses to be themselves. So long as they are not offensive or confusing, it makes for a more lively, colorful, and memorable exchange. When the jurors actually see a witness's personality, they are more likely to form an intellectual and emotional investment in your trial story and its characters.

When we discussed the pet-store case in which the manager would not allow a pregnant woman to call her husband or doctor on the store phone after she slipped and fell, or to sit at the front of the shop and wait for her ride, we said the following: "Without this jury proof, the facts that were so critically and legally important to the standing of the claim were sterile and insufficient to the jurors."[15] But when Cusimano described the same thing in a meeting, he put it like this: "Those two things put a rocket ship on what was a very weak bicycle." If you have a witness like Cusimano, by all means, don't clean him up for trial.

As for your own delivery, use detail and specific facts to help paint the picture you want the jury to see. You could say a person was born and reared in the rural south, which certainly conjures

---

[15] *See* the discussion in chapter 4, "Investigating the Facts," page 74.

up an image. But different jurors will have a different image of what you're talking about. What if, instead, you included the details in the present tense? "After school, I walk toward my house down a crooked gravel road. Although there is little traffic on the sweltering hot August day, I cover my mouth and eyes to protect them from the cloud of dust created by the lone passing car. Now, I see my house—clapboard wooden siding, bare of paint, with broken steps and two rocking chairs held together with wire and glue." When you are discussing a key point in your trial story, use descriptive language to create graphic images the jurors will carry with them during trial and into deliberations.

COMMIT TO THE STORY

There is a popular story about a thousand-legged caterpillar who is walking through the leaves, legs in perfect unison with the grace of a ballet dancer. Then the caterpillar encounters a grasshopper who asks, "How in the world do you walk with all those legs?" As soon as the caterpillar thinks about it, he trips and falls.

You cannot tell an engaging story when you are on the outside, observing yourself and wondering how you are doing. You must be in sync, in focus, and in the moment. Think out, not in. It's about your client and the jurors, not you. Lose yourself, and the jurors will follow your message along the trail of your trial story.

CASE STUDY:
REAR-END COLLISION

Now that we have outlined our basic format for developing a trial story, we thought we would show you what that looks like from start to finish in one particular case. We've selected one of Bossart's cases, a classic rear-end collision case with challenges on liability, causation, and damages.

To develop the trial story, Bossart had to seek out salient facts about the crash itself. On causation issues, he worked with an engineer to discover facts that explained the plaintiff's injuries. And on damages, he pulled together facts from lay and expert witnesses who were above suspicion. By using Bottom Up case preparation, Bossart was able to find the story behind the facts that made this a winning case.

A high school wrestling coach was driving home late at night and came to a four-way stop. As he began to drive through the intersection, an oncoming car suddenly turned left in front of him. The coach applied his brakes to avoid a crash, but the car behind rear-ended him. The oncoming car that turned left never stopped.

The coach went home without going to the doctor that night. The next day when his neck began to hurt, he visited the doctor. The X-rays the doctor took were normal and showed no sign of physical injury. But the coach's neck didn't get any better. After receiving chiropractic treatment, he was still in pain.

The coach filed a lawsuit against the driver who rear-ended him. The defendant denied fault for the crash and blamed it on the unidentified oncoming car that had turned left. In addition, the defendant claimed, the plaintiff had not been seriously hurt. The defendant's engineer testified that the defendant was driving only seven to ten miles per hour and that the impact caused no physical damage to either car. As a result, the expert testified, the plaintiff could not have suffered a physical injury.

The plaintiff's doctor testified that the coach did indeed have a serious neck injury. In addition, the plaintiff's engineer explained that a rear-end collision can cause serious physical injury to a driver even when no damage results to the car. The plaintiff's coworkers explained how his injuries affected his daily life.

Most lawyers may not have accepted this case. At first blush, it was a typical whiplash case, the kind that average jurors would call a frivolous lawsuit. In a focus group, Bossart asked participants to agree or disagree with the following statement: "Everyone who gets into a car crash seems to want to blame someone else." Sixty-five percent of the people who agreed with that statement found for the defendant. It was such a strong predictor that we suggest you consider incorporating it into your voir dire in car wreck cases.

Even though this was a rear-end collision case in which the plaintiff was completely without fault, Bossart heard this most common response during the focus group: "This defines a frivolous lawsuit." Other remarks were similarly foreboding:

"The plaintiff was just looking to sue someone."

"This was an accident."

"This is what car insurance is for."

"The cars were not going fast enough for there to be serious injuries."

"There wasn't any damage to the cars."

"The plaintiff didn't even go to the doctor right away."

"All the medical tests ruled out any injury."

The case presented challenges on every front. On liability, the defendant's trial story was that the missing driver had caused the crash by turning left at the last minute. This empty-chair defense gave the jury the option of blaming the plaintiff's injuries on an unknown driver who was not present at trial. Bossart reframed the liability issue by turning the jury's attention away from the missing car to one of the fundamental rules of driving—not to follow too close. If the defendant had not chosen to ride the plaintiff's bumper, he would have prevented the crash—even if he had not been paying enough attention to brake for the oncoming car.

This case provides a good example of why it's important to learn as many facts about a case as early as possible. Never forget your jury proof. Juries are quick to forgive a mistake like driving through an intersection on autopilot after you've been waiting for a while and a car comes out of the blue.

By asking lots of questions in discovery, you are likely to discover a reason for such inattention. Maybe the defendant was ruminating over that failed cross-court pass in last night's basketball game. He might have been on the phone arguing with his girlfriend about why he and his wife had to go away for the weekend. Or he could have just spilled a beer in his lap while admiring his new swastika tattoo. When you show jurors why the defendant was not watching the road, they are less likely to fall back on the stuff-happens bias that causes them to view the conduct as a forgivable mistake.

And the more unusual the defendant's conduct is, the more likely it is that jurors will blame him. That's our fifth commandment for overcoming jury bias—using the norm bias to your advantage. Search out facts to include in your trial story that fall outside the norm. They could be the very things that win your case.

Bossart also reframed the common jury bias about personal responsibility to spotlight the defendant's lack of it. Usually, the personal-responsibility bias causes jurors to find that the plaintiff was responsible for his own injuries. But in this case, Bossart was able to turn that around and use the bias against the defendant.

Instead of accepting responsibility for the undeniable fact that he had crashed into the back of the coach's car, the defendant tried to blame the unidentified driver who had turned left in front of the plaintiff's car. But Bossart was able to successfully argue that the other car didn't matter: The defendant shouldn't be allowed to blame his inattention and decision to follow too closely on someone else who wasn't even in the courtroom. The defendant should have accepted personal responsibility for his liability in causing the crash.

Causation was also a challenge in this case. Probably the most difficult causation issue was that no damage was done to the vehicle. For many people, this issue is determinative. And it provides an example of a good series of questions to ask during voir dire in similar cases:

Q: How many people feel that if there is no damage to the vehicle, then you can never ever suffer an injury?

[Hands go up.]

Q: No matter what the evidence is, you wouldn't believe that someone could be hurt if there is no damage to the vehicle?

A: Yes.

Q: No matter what the judge instructs?

A: That's right.

Those are panel members who should be struck for cause. And there were many with those views in the focus group for this case.

Bossart reframed the issue by shifting the jurors' focus from the undamaged car to its driver, the high school wrestling coach with invisible but painful and chronic neck injuries. To do this, he worked with a biomechanical engineer in Fargo, North Dakota, who is now internationally known for explaining these types of injuries. The expert created an easy-to-understand six-minute video that explains—through basic engineering principles—the six forces that a rear-end collision exerts on a driver's head and neck.

The video explained the unavoidable physical impact from those forces, and it answered the defendant's spurious suggestion that a collision at seven miles per hour that causes no damage to the vehicle similarly causes no injury to the driver. From an engineering standpoint, you don't need damage to the automobile. Cars today are designed to withstand a considerable impact with no damage, but the human body is not. The video explained that seeming paradox to the jurors. Always remember to orchestrate your trial story with effective videos, PowerPoints, time lines, and other demonstrative aids that help the jury quickly understand.

Bossart also had to reframe the issue of damages. Some lawyers would call the wrestling coach's case a minor-impact, soft-tissue (MIST) case. This label, however, only buys into the defendant's trial story. The impact to the plaintiff's car may have been minor, but the impact to the plaintiff was not. So Bossart used a different frame. The plaintiff was a thirty-five-year-old physical education teacher and wrestling coach. His neck injury was permanent. The pain was chronic. This was a key point because chronic pain is a major health problem in America in terms of people who are unable to work. Chronic pain often requires medication and can lead to depression, addiction, and suicide.

Bossart found a way to explain the concept of invisible, chronic pain in simple, straightforward language the jurors could understand:

> If you have a tiny pebble in your shoe, would you walk around the mall all day with that hard, little rock stabbing into the ball of your foot? No, because before long, the pain from that small pebble would be unbearable. The same is true of chronic pain in the neck or back. It's debilitating.

What else can you do to show this invisible pain to the jury without making your client look like a malingerer? You do it through other witnesses. Frame the story from the viewpoint of someone other than the plaintiff. What changes had the other teachers at school and members of the wrestling team observed? These were people who could describe the effects of the plaintiff's chronic neck pain without arousing the jurors' suspicion. Remember: Show the jury. Don't tell them.

The common jury bias of suspicion was a big obstacle in the case, as the focus groups revealed beforehand. A soft-tissue case with just $9,500 in medical bills may not be one in which most lawyers would retain a jury consultant. Yet this particular case is exactly the sort in which you need jury research. When you know in advance that one or more of the five common juror biases is likely to present a significant challenge, begin jury research early to learn how to overcome juror biases and allow jurors to root for your client.

Remember the eighth commandment: create empathy. Jurors will feel empathy for plaintiffs they can relate to. When your client is an optimist, for example, make sure that comes through in his deposition: "Yeah, I've been hurt, but for me it's a short-term thing. I'm doing everything I can to move forward with my life. These injuries are not the end of my world." If jurors see the plaintiff through the opposite lens, the "woe is me" frame, they'll have no reason to budge from their suspicion bias. But everyone loves an indomitable spirit.

And don't forget jury proof for establishing the plaintiff's credibility with the jury. This is another way to overcome suspicion. What was the coach doing on the road out late at night? Was he returning home after choir practice at church? Had he dropped off a group of Boy Scouts at school after a weekend camping trip? Or had he just run up to the store to buy orange juice for his son who was getting a cold? Was the coach really the kind of person who would make up a neck injury—or was he a solid, valued member of his community? Look for the story behind the facts.

And so this is how Bossart reframed the issues in a rear-end collision case that resulted in soft-tissue injurie. Bossart began by reframing the defendant's liability. The defendant chose to follow the plaintiff too closely and not watch the road closely enough. What's worse, the defendant refused to accept personal responsibility and tried instead to blame another driver.

On causation, Bossart overcame the suspicion bias with expert testimony to explain in layman's terms how a crash that causes no damage to a vehicle can nevertheless cause significant injuries for the driver. And on damages, he again used expert testimony to explain that chronic pain is a significant, serious injury. He showed the jury how the coach's chronic pain had affected his life by relying on coworkers and admiring students who could see and describe his health challenges. Meanwhile, the plaintiff did not pretend to be someone different than he was—an optimist who was determined not to let his injuries define his life. In this way, the jurors were able to develop empathy for a man who refused to quit.

That's how we develop an effective trial story.

WHAT WE HAVE LEARNED

Reframe Facts and Develop a Trial Story

Developing an effective trial story is the strongest weapon you have for overcoming common juror biases. With Bottom Up preparation, the emphasis is more on finding the story than telling it. You've listened to your client, investigated the facts, and done the research to learn what matters to jurors. Sift through that information until the trial story emerges—until you find the lion in the granite. To do that, apply our tools for developing an effective trial story:

◆ Follow the Jury Bias Model's Ten Commandments.
◆ Focus on the defendant.
◆ Show, don't tell.
◆ Include jury proof.
◆ Reframe facts.
◆ Establish credibility.
◆ Remember that less is better.
◆ Make it understandable and interesting.
◆ Commit to the story.

8

TESTING YOUR CASE

In a perfect world, after you develop what you believe will be a persuasive trial story, consider testing it out with a structured focus group. Testing is also important for graphic illustrations, demonstrative aids, and key witnesses.

If it's avoidable—after you spend the time, money, mental energy, and emotion to develop a workable trial story—you do not want the first time it's presented to be to a live jury. It would be like buying a beautiful old Victorian house without having it inspected first. The development of a winning trial story is critical, and testing it is also very important so your trial story can be modified if necessary. If the cost is justifiable, test it with a structured focus group. If the cost is not justifiable, test it with family, friends, and acquaintances.

Do not conduct your first focus group during post-trial interviews. Instead of waiting until your trial is over to learn whether you have a good trial story (or not), doesn't it make more sense to use focus groups when you still have time to test your theory of the case, change it, and make it more effective? Even better, think about using focus groups right at the start to test whether or not it's a case you want to take. The cost of a focus group is nothing compared to your years-long investment of time and resources during case preparation. Testing with a focus group is the proverbial ounce of prevention that's worth a pound of cure.

WHY SOME
LAWYERS RESIST TESTING

We know from experience that many of you are wondering why you need testing at this point. For us as trial consultants, one of our greatest challenges in the testing step of Bottom Up case preparation is convincing our clients that they actually need it. There are three reasons why lawyers often fail to test their trial story before trying it out on the jury.

THEY ARE UNAWARE

First, some lawyers—including very good lawyers—are simply unaware of the benefits of focus groups and the need to test for possible weaknesses in the preparation of their cases. They were successful in the past, so why not now? Well, times have changed, jurors have changed, and we must change as well. These are the lawyers who tell us things like this: "You know, I really have no idea what happened. The case tried beautifully. Everything worked. The judge let all the evidence in. My client did a wonderful job. I have no earthly idea why I lost." We understand because we used to be just like these lawyers.

Before he and Wenner started researching juror bias for ATLA in the 1990s, Cusimano had no idea that he needed to test his trial story before the jury heard it. He still cringes when he recalls a case that a defense lawyer referred to him decades ago. The defendant, a wealthy power company, made a substantial settlement offer, which the referring lawyer encouraged the client to reject. Everyone agreed the case tried beautifully—including Cusimano and the defense lawyer who referred the case. The judge predicted that Cusimano would break every damages record in the county and possibly the state. While the jury was out, Cusimano reached out to his opposing counsel, who was looking glum:

> "What's wrong, Counselor?"
> "Do you know about the thing we do annually at the Defense Lawyers Conference?"
> "No."
> "If anybody gets a million-dollar defense verdict against him, he has to walk up to the front of the room and they put a commode lid over his head and make him wear it all day. I'm going to get a commode lid on my head."

Cusimano was feeling pretty good when the jury came back in. The foreperson read the verdict: "We, the ladies and gentlemen of the jury, find the issues in favor of the plaintiff. And assess damages at zero."

As Cusimano struggled for breath, the judge polled the jury and then entered the jury room to explain that the jurors must have intended to rule for the defendant. But they insisted: "Absolutely not! We wanted to rule for the plaintiff, but we don't want to assess any damages."

Fortunately for the client, Cusimano succeeded in having the verdict reversed on appeal. But Cusimano learned then and there that decades of successful trial experience are not enough to accurately predict what a jury will do.

HUBRIS

The second reason that some lawyers choose not to test their trial story is overconfidence. These lawyers remind Lazarus, who was a leading Democratic campaign strategist before becoming a trial consultant, of a few congressional candidates he worked for years ago. Occasionally, he would encounter a candidate who was resistant to the idea of doing polling and research for a campaign. One of these defiant candidates once pronounced, "Any politician worth his salt knows the issues in his constituency." Well, that was the last term he served in Congress. The bottom line is that we, and the lawyers we work with, do not know all the issues. Every case we work on, we're always surprised by something we learn. Every time.

TOO INVESTED IN THEIR TRIAL STORY

The third reason that lawyers are reluctant to test their trial story is that they can't bear to part with it. Just like the panel members on your jury who have already formed an opinion of your client before you ever say a word in voir dire, lawyers also create stories of what their clients' cases are about. Once people form beliefs, they don't want to let go. That's as true for lawyers as it is for jurors.[1] In fact, lawyers may be even more fixed in their beliefs than jurors. By the time the trial date approaches, lawyers have invested considerable time, energy, money, and other resources into the case. They cannot easily let go of their views.

---

[1] Roy F. Baumeister and Kathleen D. Vohs, eds., *Encyclopedia of Social Psychology* (Los Angeles: SAGE Publications, 2007), 109–110.

Nobody Gets Anything Right the First Time

Nobody gets anything right the first time. It doesn't work that way in real life. No one swings a baseball bat the right way the first time. No one hits a perfect serve the first time she picks up a tennis racket. And think about the first time you had to ask someone out on a date. Everything new in life—we don't get it perfect the first time.

So what's the likelihood that you would get your trial story right the first time? Why would you even expect to? That's why you have to test it and evaluate it based on the data you have. Each time you significantly modify the trial story, if at all possible, retest it and keep reworking it until you get it right.

How to Test Your Trial Story

Testing your trial story or any other part of your case is a labor-intensive process. Ideally, you would approach testing in much the same way that you would conduct your initial jury research. In Bottom Up case preparation, you should use focus groups whenever the case merits it.

If you've already done concept focus groups as part of earlier jury research, then in the testing phase, you should use structured focus groups instead. You give a presentation that includes both facts and argument and is similar to a closing argument. Another lawyer makes the defendant's presentation. You present a short rebuttal. Then the group deliberates. As we discussed earlier,[2] a

---

[2] *See* the discussion in chapter 5, "Conducting Jury Research," page 91.

structured focus group is great for testing your trial story. Win or lose, you may not know why unless you spend time afterward with the focus-group participants to explore why they made the decisions they did.

At the end of the last focus group, sit down and ask, "What did we learn? What did we hear that surprised us?" Many lawyers are shocked into the realization that they need to modify their trial story. And that's the whole purpose of testing, to learn what works and what doesn't.

If you can, hire a court reporter to provide a transcript of the focus group and record it on video as it's taking place. That gives you the opportunity to come back, study, and learn something from it. Look at what the focus-group respondents have told you, and follow their lead. That's the best way to learn how to hone an existing trial story or start all over and develop a better one.

Once you've shaped your trial story and tested it out to ensure you're on the right track, if the case justifies it, mini mock trials are effective for exploring the jury's likely reaction to your opening statement, closing argument, key witness, or trial exhibits. Again, as with a structured focus group, sit down with the mock jurors afterward to get their feedback on specific issues.

With each round of focus groups, or other methods of testing, you're making progress toward a trial story that is more credible and raises less suspicion. You're working toward a point where focus-group participants are less willing to blame the plaintiff, where they are more interested in the plaintiff's well-being than in their own. When you've finally reached the point where the focus-group participants understand the story and agree with it because it's consistent with their beliefs, you'll know you likely have a winner.

What we have just described, of course, is the ideal way to test out a trial story. In actuality, many lawyers we consult with worry that they don't have the time or resources to test their trial story with several focus groups. Lawyers often contact us when they are no more than a month from trial and they have one nagging issue that their trial story won't accommodate. At that point in time, it's true that changing everything up will likely create disorder and panic. But you can still benefit from testing your trial story with a focus group to learn how to best frame the issues.

For attorneys who have never witnessed a well-run focus group, the experience is mind altering. Remember that the purpose of testing your trial story with a focus group is to hear everything—the good, the bad, and the ugly. Some successful trial lawyers have difficulty understanding that the purpose of a focus group is not to win. Indeed, you learn a lot more by losing than you do by winning. You can't figure out what it takes to win a case until you see what will make you lose it. It's startling for lawyers to learn how ordinary people perceive the facts in cases the lawyers thought they themselves understood so well.

CASE EXAMPLE: TESTING THE TRIAL STORY

Testing the trial story was critical in a traumatic brain injury case we consulted on in Boston. The plaintiff's lawyer brought us in early to work on the case—two years before trial. This was ideal because it allowed us to conduct jury research to find the problems in the case, and it gave the trial lawyer time to go back to the facts and develop the evidence he needed to defuse those issues.

When we got involved, the known facts were these: A group of five people were drinking at a Boston bar when someone else attempted to sit on a bar stool that members of the group had been using. A confrontation ensued in which one member of the group asked the newcomer to move down the bar. In the surveillance video, the newcomer did not appear belligerent but the management did move him to a different location. The newcomer then used his mobile phone to make a call. Sometime later, two iron-pumping hulks joined their buddy at the bar.

At the end of the night, when the two groups left the bar, a fight began on the street out in front. It was unclear who threw the first punch. Some witnesses suggested it was the plaintiff, while others disagreed. In any event, the plaintiff received a permanent traumatic brain injury as a result.

The most troubling issue we identified with focus groups involved personal responsibility. When the first encounter began, the plaintiff's group of friends were in a confrontation with someone who was alone at the time. Later, the plaintiff may have been the one to throw the first punch. A jury could easily decide that the plaintiff's injuries were his own fault.

Remember step one of Bottom Up case preparation: investigate the facts and never leave them. When our trial lawyer client went back to the facts, he was able to discover helpful evidence.

First, the plaintiff was not even with his friends when they argued over the bar stool. He was in the restroom at the time. And when the ostensibly innocent newcomer made the phone call shown on the bar surveillance video, he was in fact inviting his muscle-bound friends to join him in solidarity at the bar. These were helpful facts, but they would not prevent jurors from holding the plaintiff accountable for the behavior of his friends. If he was such a great guy, why was the plaintiff hanging out with people who would get involved in a verbal altercation with a stranger over a bar stool?

Further, jurors do not like to be asked to protect a man from himself. Jurors believe you should not place yourself in a dangerous situation. Jurors will want to know things like this: Why didn't the plaintiff and his friends just walk away? How long had they been there? (They had been there a long time.) How much had they had to drink? (They'd had quite a lot.) And also, what was the plaintiff doing there in the first place? And those are the accursed words: "in the first place." Any time your trial story elicits that language from focus-group participants, you have a problem.

A trial story about a street fight over a bar stool focuses attention on the plaintiff's conduct and leaves too much to the imagination. Was it a rundown bar in a bad neighborhood? (It was a high-end bar on a fashionable street.) Was he a drunken construction worker who probably has an offensive bumper sticker on his truck? (He owned a successful business.) The minute the judge tells the panel members that the case is about a fight in a bar, these are the questions racing through the potential jurors' minds. The brain injury case in Boston had to be about the bar (the defendant) and not the bar stool.

What was the responsibility of the bar management? What should a manager do when any kind of conflict occurs? Did the bar management do what it should have? That was where the focus had to be; that was the trial story. We used our focus group to test the bar's safety rules and protocols, then built the case around those.

Over the course of six focus groups, we reframed the case from one about an argument over a bar stool to one about the bar's responsibility for making the premises safe. By never leaving the facts, we found some very helpful evidence. A video surveillance tape from later in the night, when the two groups left the bar, showed that everyone—the bar manager, the bouncer, and the bar patrons—all rushed outside because they knew there would be a fight. The bouncer wasn't separating anyone; he and the manager didn't even try to restrain anyone. They were all more interested in watching the fight.

The facts also made it clear that bar management knew the fight was likely to occur. When the weightlifters arrived at the bar to help their friend, the bar manager asked, "You aren't here to start any trouble, are you?" Bar owners know people are likely to engage in aggressive behavior in a bar, especially after they have been drinking. It's entirely foreseeable. That's why bars should have procedures in place to prevent fights over a bar stool long before they occur. But in the Boston case, bar management was more interested in viewing the spectacle than preventing or stopping it.

It wasn't until our third set of focus groups that we actually tested the trial story we had developed. By then, we had done enough research that the last focus groups were structured, rather than concept, focus groups. We wanted the assurance that we had it right. We took what we learned from those final structured focus groups and made a few tweaks to the trial story.

Our client, who did an excellent job building this case throughout, won the case at trial and received a very favorable verdict from the jury. The final tweaks to the trial story after the last structured focus group resulted in the jurors apportioning more liability to the defendant bar (90 percent on the defendant, with 5 percent on the assailant, and only 5 percent on the plaintiff) than did the last focus-group respondents.

This was a trial that our client spent more than two years preparing. Depositions, motions for summary judgment, expert witness fees—none of that makes a bit of difference if you don't have a trial story jurors believe in. Our client understood that testing his trial story with focus groups, listening to the findings, and learning the lessons the groups had to teach were as important as any other step in preparing that traumatic brain injury case for trial.

CASE EXAMPLE: TESTING EXHIBITS

In one of Wenner's cases, he relied on testing to discover that one of the key exhibits he planned to use at trial was not at all effective. This is the case we described earlier that involved a young woman in her twenties who collapsed while riding a stationary bicycle in the University of Arizona recreation center.[3]

---

[3] *See* the discussion in Chapter 5, "Conducting Jury Research," page 105.

The lawsuit alleged that if the student employees working at the center had been trained in CPR and had performed it, the young woman would not have suffered a brain injury.

The week before trial, Wenner was in his sixth focus group. He began his opening statement using a large graphic that displayed a university brochure featuring the state-of-the-art recreation center. The point of the exhibit was to illustrate how much the school had spent on fancy equipment and how little it had spent on training.

When the focus-group participants deliberated, they did indeed remember the exhibit. But what caught their attention was this: Nowhere in the brochure did the school ever promise that the recreation center employees were trained in CPR. Wenner created the exhibit only to show how much the school had spent on elaborate equipment, but what the focus group saw was no guarantee that the people working there were CPR-certified.

Obviously, Wenner trashed the exhibit. But the larger issue is that even an experienced trial lawyer—one who worked with Cusimano to develop the Jury Bias Model—could not have predicted the focus group's reaction to that exhibit. By testing it in advance, Wenner learned that the exhibit could only hurt him at trial.

LEARNING FROM TESTING

The most important words in the preceding sentence are "Wenner learned." The whole purpose for testing is to learn. Sometimes, you learn that your trial story is great and just needs a few tweaks. You might need to change the order in which you present things or emphasize one piece of evidence over another. Other times, testing reveals that the trial story you are wedded to will not bear fruit.

Not surprisingly, many confident trial lawyers are not easily uncoupled from a trial story they're enamored with. Many are unrealistically optimistic about the merits of their case. We tend to cling to preexisting notions about what the trial story should be. But testing is valuable only if you are willing to listen to and learn from the results.

Years ago, Wenner was conducting a focus group for a trial lawyer who refused to hear a focus group's rejection of her trial story. One of the participants suffered a heart attack during the focus group. As the paramedics wheeled him from the building, Wenner's trial-lawyer client followed alongside the stretcher, notebook in hand, still trying to persuade the ashen-faced man of her view of the case.

Cusimano remembers working with an excellent trial lawyer who was equally committed to his particular trial story for his client's case, despite what testing revealed. They lost with the first focus group. They lost again with the second. The trial lawyer complained to Cusimano: "We'd never get a jury like this. The focus groups didn't understand the case. They just bought into the defense."

Because the lawyer was a close friend, Cusimano proposed another chance: "You pay the cost of a third focus group, and I won't charge you for my time. You argue the plaintiff's case alone, and we won't even put on a defense. Let's see if the trial story works then." After losing with the third focus group, the trial lawyer was finally convinced of what the testing plainly showed—the lawyer needed a new trial story.

We took a different approach in another very large Alabama case in which a team of trial lawyers represented the plaintiffs. The case was not testing well with focus groups, but the trial lawyers couldn't accept that the problem was their trial story. We understand that this is much easier for us to digest than for our clients. A skilled trial lawyer who makes a practice of using focus groups may have participated in dozens of them. But a skilled trial consultant may have conducted hundreds, if not thousands. That experience can teach how to quickly assess when a trial story needs work. It's not that consultants have a silver bullet; we don't. But our more objective viewpoint allows us to see how the plaintiff's story can best be told—or at least where to start.

We persuaded the trial lawyers in the Alabama case to let us write the best two-page trial story we could using our recommended approach. We also created the strongest possible two-page story for the defendant. When we read those two trial stories to a focus group, participants started to go the plaintiffs' way. That's what persuaded the lawyers on the trial team that they needed a new trial story.

The case was not a shaky one. In fact, there was so much evidence to support the plaintiffs' case that it was rock solid. The evidence contained thousands of bookkeeping entries and transactions, involving hundreds of millions of dollars. That was the difficulty. The lawyers couldn't help themselves from crushing the focus groups' interest by piling on every single bit of helpful evidence. It made for a very dull and ultimately confusing story.

This is why testing your trial story is critical, even when you've done a good amount of jury research to begin with. Most trial lawyers would not expect to lose a good case by presenting too much evidence. Many don't understand the pitfalls of information overload. This is especially true in large, complex cases. Confusion is the defendant's best friend. No matter the intricacies, your trial story must be clear, credible, and consistent. If it's not, the time to find that out is in testing with a focus group—before you're in trial with the jury. Don't dilute your message with too much information. There is impact and wisdom in keeping it simple.

WHAT WE HAVE LEARNED
Test & Modify Your Case

Testing your trial story with focus groups is a critical step in developing your case for trial using Bottom Up case preparation. Plaintiff's trial work is expensive. By the time you reach trial, you've invested considerable time, money, energy, and emotion in your case. You wouldn't make any other investment of that magnitude without conducting due diligence. Your client's lawsuit should be no different. Keep these points in mind:

◆ Most lawyers who are reluctant to take advantage of focus groups to test their trial story are either unaware of the benefits of focus groups or are overinvested in the story they've developed.

◆ The best way to test your trial story is with structured focus groups or mini mock trials, after which you visit with participants to hear their feedback.

◆ Testing is essential for cases involving known juror biases, as in the Boston traumatic brain injury case in which personal responsibility was an issue. Testing revealed that the trial story the jurors believed in centered on the bar's choice not to manage foreseeable conflicts between groups of drinking patrons.

◆ Testing also demonstrates which trial exhibits are more likely to hurt than help.

◆ Testing is effective only when you listen to and learn from it.

9

UNDERSTANDING AND APPLYING BELIEFS

Everyone has deeply held beliefs. One of the central aims of Bottom Up case preparation is to discover and understand those beliefs and apply them for the plaintiff's ultimate benefit.

When we think of strongly held beliefs, it's easy to focus on religion or politics. But we humans do not limit our strong beliefs to those two categories. Lazarus, for example, is a Washington, DC, resident who hates the local NFL team. Every year after another disappointing season, he is bewildered to read a *Washington Post* column bemoaning, "Had we only made it into the playoffs this year, we would have won the Super Bowl because we match up so much better against all these other teams." He and millions of others around the globe have very deeply held beliefs about football, including beliefs about what "football" means.

Here's the thing about beliefs—they're hard to change. Dick Cheney still claims there were weapons of mass destruction in Iraq in 2003. And it took a majority of the rest of the country four or five years to accept that Colin Powell was wrong when he told us there were.

Beliefs can be powerful obstacles. Do not ignore them. Instead, use focus groups to make yourself aware of jurors' beliefs. Then work to understand them and present your case in such a way that jurors recognize your trial story as consistent with their beliefs. In addition, examine your own beliefs in case they are blinding you to everyone else's.

Jurors' Beliefs

Once you know what jurors' likely beliefs about your case are, you can work to understand them and, ideally, incorporate them into your trial story. At a minimum, you can plan to sidestep the beliefs that are troublesome. As you develop a strategy for dealing with jurors' beliefs, remember these four observations:

1. Jurors' beliefs won't change during trial.
2. Jurors are suspicious.
3. Jurors cannot listen to and comprehend everything.
4. Jurors will not listen to facts that contradict their beliefs.

Jurors' Beliefs Won't Change During Trial

The first thing to understand about jurors' beliefs is that they are not going anywhere. Trial lawyers often wonder what they can do to change someone's beliefs. Our response? Nothing. Maybe a blind tent revivalist from Mississippi can change beliefs, but for the rest of us, no.

Think about how beliefs are truly formed, with repeated support from different sources affirming those beliefs over a long period of time. At some point, things transform in people's minds from something they believe to something they *know*. Once a belief is that deeply held, research shows that the believer, even when presented with evidence that the facts underlying the belief are wrong, will cling to the belief.[1] As counterintuitive as it is, the contradictory evidence only strengthens a person's beliefs.[2]

There is nothing wrong with jurors having beliefs that will not favor your client. In fact, it is almost impossible to imagine a circumstance where jurors won't have some belief that works to your client's disadvantage. The problem occurs when jurors decide the case based on beliefs that hurt you rather than those that help you. Your job is to find a way to present the case that triggers jurors' beliefs that are helpful to the cause, rather than dwelling on an effort to convince jurors to change beliefs that harm the cause. Trying to convince jurors to change a belief only tells them that this issue is an important one they should focus on.

In many areas of our lives, we encounter situations where we are either witness to efforts, or are tempted to make our own efforts, to "correct" people's "misguided" or "uninformed" beliefs. Political campaigns often try to persuade voters that the candidate, who leads a privileged life as a powerful decision maker, is

---

[1] Charles G. Lord, Lee Ross, and Mark R. Lepper, "Biased Assimilation and Attitude Polarization: The Effects of Prior Theories on Subsequently Considered Evidence," *Journal of Personality and Social Psychology* 37, no. 11 (1979): 2098–2109. (People persist in their beliefs even after the evidence is discredited.)

[2] Brendan Nyhan and Jason Reifler, "When Corrections Fail: The Persistence of Political Misperceptions" *Political Behavior* 32, no. 2 (June 2010): 303–330, https://doi.org/10.1007/s11109-010-9112-2; Brendan Nyhan, Ethan Porter, Jason Reifler, and Thomas Wood, "Taking Corrections Literally But Not Seriously? The Effects of Information on Factual Beliefs and Candidate Favorability." (June 29, 2017). Available at SSRN: https://ssrn.com/abstract=2995128. (Facts may change beliefs but not attitudes or behavior); Thomas Wood and Ethan Porter, "The Elusive Backfire Effect: Mass Attitudes' Steadfast Factual Adherence" *Political Behavior* (January 2018): 1–16, https://doi.org/10.1007/s11109-018-9443-y.

just a down-to-earth, golly-shucks person like all the rest of us. Just check out the ads in any congressional campaign. Or see the efforts of Mitt Romney's 2012 presidential campaign to persuade voters that his heart was with the middle class.

Through the course of the 2012 presidential campaign, the more Romney focused on how much he understood and was devoted to the middle class, the more voters favored Barack Obama. Rather than changing voters' beliefs about who Romney was, Romney succeeded in emphasizing one of the issues where he was weakest by comparison to Obama—his distance from the day-to-day life experience of typical Americans.

Recall the revelation of Romney's embarrassing statement at a fundraiser, where he said he was giving up on 47 percent of the electorate who don't pay income taxes and therefore believe in a country full of entitlements and handouts. The Romney campaign floundered as it tried to figure out what to do. The Obama campaign knew this was a statement that confirmed many voters' worst fears about Romney—that he was anything but a friend of people who work for a paycheck and receive a W-2 for the taxes they have had withheld. At first, Romney tried to reaffirm the virtue of his original comment, saying only that he stated it inelegantly.

After polls showed Romney sliding as a result of his original statement about the 47 percent, Romney changed tactics and decided to directly take on his seeming distance from the middle-class experience. He gave a speech insisting that he really did care about the middle class and released an ad that stated, in part, "President Obama and I both care about poor and middle-class families." All of this effort by Romney focused voters' attention on the issue of whether or not Romney cared about the middle class.

As a millionaire hundreds of times over who prided himself on his concern about the bottom line, whether he cared about the poor and middle class was not a question the Romney campaign could win. Polls showed that between five to seven times as many voters in swing states felt Romney's policies would favor the rich versus the middle class.[3]

By contrast, Romney could have been campaigning on the deficit or on the question of whether the economy would be likely to improve under Obama's stewardship. On both of those questions, Romney had a fighting chance as the same swing state polls showed he was more or less even with Obama. Instead, Romney allowed his focus to shift and spent precious resources telling voters that the critical issue in the campaign was whether or not he was concerned about the middle class. In other words, Romney focused voters' attention on an issue where voters had developed a belief that worked to Romney's disadvantage. By hammering away at this issue and trying to change voters' beliefs, Romney told voters that this was an important issue they should use when deciding how to vote.

In 2016, by comparison, Republican nominee Donald Trump made no effort to pretend he was a man of the people. Instead, he asserted that his great wealth was a sign that he knew how to get things done, meaning he could help working people in a way his opponent, Hillary Clinton, could not. Clinton's wealth, in the Trump narrative, was based on her corruption, while Trump's wealth was based on know-how and hard work. Thus, someone

---

[3] *See* the *New York Times* polling series in Florida, Ohio, Pennsylvania, Wisconsin, Colorado, and Virginia during the month of September 2012. In the closest margin, 56 percent of Virginia voters thought Romney's policies would favor the wealthy, versus 11 percent who thought his policies would favor the middle class (a 5:1 ratio). At the other extreme, 56 percent of Florida voters thought Romney's policies would favor the rich, versus 8 percent who thought he would favor the middle class (a 7:1 ratio). By contrast, the same polls found that the number who felt Obama's policies would favor the rich was 10 percent in Wisconsin and only in single digits in Florida, Ohio, Pennsylvania, Colorado, and Virginia. In all of the target states the *New York Times* polled during September 2012, more than 80 percent (and most typically about 85 percent) were relatively evenly divided across Obama's policies favoring the middle class, favoring the poor, or treating everyone the same.

claiming to be one of the wealthiest people in the world was able to win over working-class voters and forge a historic upset on Election Day.

Even when politics arise in casual conversation among friends, one person often tries to persuade the other of views on whether raising or lowering taxes will or will not create more jobs. If you, the reader, have ever watched a conversation like that, you probably noticed (and shook your head in wonder) that facts and data do not alter perceptions on this issue. Belief in either the panacea of lower taxes or redistributive benefits of higher taxes is set in people's minds by the time they reach adulthood, and facts are not going to change their views.

If you find the task of shaking people's political beliefs to be difficult, try persuading a sports fan that his or her favorite team isn't quite as good as the fan believes it is. As referenced earlier in this chapter, there have been times in Washington, DC, when many a Redskins fan was convinced the team would have been a lock to win the Super Bowl, but for the fact the team wasn't good enough to make the playoffs.[4] The reality that the team was unable to qualify for postseason play did not dissuade fans from the belief that the Redskins were good enough to be Super Bowl champions. It is that kind of irrational thought process that results from the very human process of holding to a belief.

Following their heydays in the 1980s and early 1990s, it took years and years of misery for Redskins fans to come around to believing their team was no longer one of the best in the NFL. Compare the years it took for a belief about the Redskins to

---

[4] In the interest of full disclosure, one of the authors is a dedicated 49ers fan who loathes the Redskins in no small part because of their fans' irrational beliefs. However, one of the other authors of this book has been known to be just as irrational about the Alabama Crimson Tide as Redskins fans are about their favorite franchise. And the lawyer who handled the bar case described in the previous chapter, an intelligent and otherwise rational human being, inexplicably clings to the irrational notion that the Patriots have been among the best teams in the NFL for at least the past decade.

change in the face of overwhelming, incontrovertible evidence (either the team can put together a winning season or it can't) to the relatively brief time attorneys have in front of a jury to try to change beliefs with contested evidence about which jurors are suspicious. If jurors spent a lifetime developing a belief system, no attorney is going to change it over the course of a trial.

The problem with trying to persuade people about the error of their beliefs is that beliefs are not malleable. Our beliefs do not depend on an objective assessment of facts and a rational thought process. Our beliefs are the result of a lifetime of experience and interpretation which, rather than being subject to objective fact analysis, creates a selective prism through which we filter facts. People do not alter beliefs to fit a set of facts. Rather, people in all contexts and all walks of life selectively choose and interpret facts to fit their beliefs.

Now think about your own cases. You have a choice between hammering away at a topic where you start on losing ground and your chances of changing anyone's belief are slim to none, or finding something else on which to focus jurors' attention. Would you rather spend time emphasizing the importance of a harmful belief, or would you rather spend your time getting jurors focused on a different belief—one that favors your client?

In reality, some beliefs are more fundamental (core beliefs) than others and are harder to change. Other beliefs are more peripheral. But once the belief is present, changing it is an uphill, near vertical, climb. The easiest thing to do when communicating with a juror (or anyone else, for that matter) is to reinforce an existing, salient belief. All you are doing is echoing something that your audience already has in mind. The next easiest thing to do is to draw out a latent belief—a belief that your audience holds but did not have in mind at the moment. And the next easiest thing to do after that is to fill an empty head—create a belief where none currently exists.

But the most difficult task is to change a current belief. If your case hinges on changing your jurors' core beliefs, you should accept any settlement offer that you receive and count your blessings. If your case hinges on reinforcing beliefs that are fundamental to jurors, your opposing counsel should run and hide.

REMEMBER THAT JURORS ARE SUSPICIOUS

Never forget that jurors, like the rest of us, do not like to feel that they are the targets of a sales pitch. Any overt attempt to persuade is subject to suspicion. It doesn't matter how you disguise it or what words you use. If jurors feel that you're trying to sell them something, they'll become suspicious. The best you can do is influence jurors by telling the right trial story with the salient facts in a concise manner.

JURORS CANNOT LISTEN TO EVERYTHING

Jurors are more likely to see the connection between your trial story and their beliefs if you are concise. Why is this so? First, jurors cannot listen to everything they hear during trial. It doesn't matter whether you are selling a candidate, toothpaste, or a lawsuit, most people are not that interested until the moment they have to make a decision. That's why you need a specific, simple, concise message that they hear over and over again throughout the trial. When jurors tune in, they need to hear that message and understand it quickly before they zone back out. When it's time to make a decision at the end of the case, they'll be able to sift through the detritus they vaguely recall and locate your message.

Remember that jurors are conditioned by television to expect what Bossart calls the *McTrial*, in which major capital crimes are solved, tried, and appealed in under an hour. Bossart learned this lesson when a judge in Moorhead, Minnesota, told him the trial had to be completed in three days instead of five. Much to Bossart's dismay, he was forced to call fewer witnesses and produce less evidence, and could only include the essential facts, witnesses, and evidence. The result was a nice verdict for the plaintiff, and was the birth of what he calls the McTrial.

As trial consultants, we ask lawyers to summarize their cases for us in two to three pages. Many protest: "You don't understand; we've got four experts." Still, our job is to encourage trial lawyers to pare down the information until jurors can listen and understand. If you cannot get four interested trial consultants to listen to your evidence, you cannot expect a jury to do it for free. Take the time to make your message memorable.

Finally, the science confirms what we observed in our research for ATLA and in our practice as trial consultants. Thinking is hard work physically. Your blood pressure rises, your heart rate speeds up, your pupils dilate, and your brain starts to consume glucose.[5] How long do you think jurors will remain actively engaged in the hard work of thinking about your case when they're not that interested and they're not really being paid to be? Most of the time, jurors operate on automatic. To assume they will expend a lot of effort thinking about a long and complicated trial story is naive at best. The link between your trial story and jurors' beliefs should be clear and concise.

---

[5] Ewan C. McNay, Thomas M. Fries, and Paul E. Gold, "Decreases in Rat Extracellular Hippocampal Glucose Concentration Associated with Cognitive Demand during a Spatial Task," *Proceedings of the National Academy of Sciences of the United States of America* 97, no. 6 (March, 2000), 2881–2885.

Jurors Are Partisan

It's a myth that jurors suspend judgment until the end of a trial, that they sift through all the facts like jigsaw puzzle pieces fitting together to create the picture that you see. It doesn't happen.

Jurors enter the courtroom with firmly fixed beliefs. They listen primarily for information that is consistent with the beliefs they already have. When jurors hear your trial story, they modify it to comport with their beliefs. They use facts that are consistent with the trial story they have in their heads, based on the beliefs they came in with. It's not the same trial story you told. That's why it's important to understand jurors' beliefs long before you get in the courtroom. If you tell jurors a story and expect them just to agree with you, you and your client are likely to be disappointed. Instead, frame the evidence in a way that fits with jurors' preexisting views.

Case Example: Ignoring Jurors' Beliefs

One mistake many trial lawyers make is to ignore jurors' beliefs entirely. This happens most commonly when the trial lawyer believes the facts are so strong, the evidence is so overwhelming, that the case is an obvious win. We see this all the time. The trial lawyer assumes the jurors will view the facts the way she does. And that's wrong. People do not make decisions based only on facts. They make decisions based on beliefs and life experiences and then rationalize their decisions. The facts don't matter if your jurors have core beliefs that are inconsistent with those facts.

We consulted on a medical negligence case in which the defendant doctor altered the medical records after the fact to cover his mistakes. An FBI handwriting expert testified that the records had been altered at a later time with a different pen. The defendant's negligence left his young patient a quadriplegic. The trial lawyer was convinced that he could not lose the case on these facts.

Focus-group participants didn't view the doctor's alteration of the records the same way our client did. Their response? "What did you expect the doctor to do? Say that he's responsible and to give the plaintiff all the money he wants?" They shrugged their shoulders like it was nothing. The focus-group participants agreed that the young quadriplegic's situation was tragic. But they did not see it as a justification for a large damages award. Instead, they asked, "What's the money going to do? He's going to be the same no matter what." The facts in this case appeared compelling on liability and damages, but many focus-group respondents' beliefs prevented them from finding for the plaintiff.

The focus group saw the doctor's misconduct as normal human behavior. This belief brings into play our fifth commandment involving the norm bias. Jurors need to view the defendant's conduct as a gross deviation from the norm, not as consistent with the norm. Normal behavior is forgivable behavior.

We once read a survey that showed that a majority of doctors would alter medical records to relieve themselves from liability. Many trial lawyers we knew viewed the results as beneficial for medical negligence cases. But Cusimano and Wenner predicted—unfortunately, accurately—that the general public would become so inured to the practice that jurors would accept it as normal and shrug it off. In fact, Wenner faced the issue in one of his own cases in which the defendant doctor went back into the records and filled them in to cover himself. Wenner thought it would be a major factor in the case, but, in fact, focus-group participants weren't troubled. They reasoned: "Doctors are busy. They do that; it's not unusual."

CASE EXAMPLE:
WORKING WITH JURORS' BELIEFS

Louise Logan was driving her SUV down a two-lane rural high-way when a sixty-five-foot-long, double trailer truck pulled out from a field in front of her. Louise was unable to avoid the truck. Experts for both the defense and plaintiff agreed she was moving at fifty-five miles per hour at the time of impact. The force of the collision was enough to knock the seventy-five-thousand-pound truck into the other lane of traffic. Louise sustained a debilitating fracture of her hip socket, a fractured elbow, and a fractured wrist that required the use of a plate to stabilize it.

Louise's attorney recognized that even in seemingly routine motor vehicle litigation, unanticipated issues could derail his client's case. That is why he contacted Winning Works to conduct online focus groups. While not as strong a tool as traditional in-person focus groups, online groups provide a great value for the money.

In Louise's case, the online focus groups revealed very strong beliefs that she must have been speeding. In fact, the evidence on Louise's speed was mixed. But no matter how we presented the evidence on this point, focus-group participants stuck to the belief that Louise was exceeding the speed limit.

This situation is not unique. Jurors bring a lifetime of experience and resulting belief systems to any case they hear. It is the norm that some of those beliefs will work against your client. Unfortunately, attorneys too often feel their job at trial is to change jurors' beliefs in order to prevail.

Louise's attorney was smart enough to understand he was not going to be able to win the case for her by convincing jurors that she was not speeding. So, Louise's attorney essentially conceded the issue. In his opening, he stated that there would be some evidence that Louise exceeded the speed limit, and if jurors decided that evidence was persuasive, so be it.

Rather than spending valuable time discrediting the belief that Louise was speeding, the attorney used the focus group's revelation and, instead, spent his time focusing jurors' attention on issues that would trigger beliefs friendlier to his client. In her own testimony, Louise told the truth as she knew it, and no doubt gained the confidence of jurors because her testimony was so credible.

She stated that if someone had evidence that she was speeding, she wouldn't argue with it. She didn't feel like she was speeding as she drove down the deserted country highway, but neither was she looking at the speedometer. So, she didn't really know. By treating this topic frankly and casually, Louise and her attorney conveyed to the jury that whether she was speeding wasn't really important.

What was important was whether truckers (or anyone else, for that matter) ought to look before pulling out onto a highway and double-check as they are pulling out to make sure the road remains clear. The evidence presented in this case was that, regardless of Louise's speed, she would have been in plain sight of the truck driver before his truck reached the highway, had he only been looking. The defense presented their study of the truck driver's sight lines, presumably in an effort to persuade jurors that Louise must have been traveling so fast that she was not in the truck driver's view when he first checked the road. But in fact, their own study of the sight lines showed that the truck driver had ample opportunity—five to seven seconds—to double-check the highway traffic as he pulled out, and could have stopped in plenty of time to prevent the collision.

The defense produced an expert who testified that once the truck driver did his initial check of the highway traffic—looking left, then right, then left again—and had decided the road was clear and he could start moving, he had the right of way and had no further responsibility to scan the road for traffic. This is despite the fact that the seventy-five-thousand-pound truck leaving the field from a dead stop took four seconds from the time it started moving to the time it even reached the edge of the paved surface. Louise's attorney knew from the focus groups that jurors would form a belief on this issue as well. Jurors would decide that the truck driver had an obligation to continue scanning the roadway for as long as it took to get his truck onto the road.

So, focus groups revealed that jurors would come to two conclusions in this case—that Louise was speeding and that the truck driver had an obligation to look more than once as he pulled his truck off of a field onto a rural highway. The critical decision Louise's attorney made was about which belief jurors should focus on when they deliberated over this case. Should jurors be thinking about whether Louise was speeding, or should jurors be thinking about whether the truck driver should have continued to scan the highway for traffic? Obviously, the choice Louise's attorney made—the right choice—was to make the case about the truck driver's failure to scan the highway. In the end, in part because of the decision not to try to change jurors' minds about Louise's speed (in addition to many other correct decisions our client made in his advocacy for Louise), the attorney obtained an excellent result for his client. Jurors found that the truck driver was 100 percent responsible for the injuries to Louise.

Regardless of the origin of the trial story jurors settle on, once they have a story in mind, they are highly likely to stick to it. As mentioned earlier in this chapter (as well as in the chapters on the Jury Bias Model), they will then use facts selectively. Jurors will latch on to evidence that supports their version of the story and discount or entirely ignore evidence that runs counter to their version of the story.

With the importance of framing and the trial story in mind, consider again the first paragraph from this example. For your convenience, it appears below:

Louise Logan was driving her SUV down a two-lane rural highway when a sixty-five-foot-long, double-trailer truck pulled out from a field in front of her. Louise was unable to avoid the truck. Experts for both the defense and plaintiff agreed she was moving at fifty-five miles per hour at the time of impact. The force of the collision was enough to knock the seventy-five-thousand-pound truck into the other lane of traffic. Louise sustained a debilitating fracture of her hip socket, a fractured elbow, and a fractured wrist that required the use of a plate to stabilize it.

The initial framing of this story is not accidental. For the purposes of this chapter, the case is stated in a way that initially has the reader thinking about Louise Logan. The likely result of that framing is the reader may well have come to the conclusion, after reading just that one paragraph, that Louise was speeding. In other words, the framing of the case was changed to guide the reader to the same conclusion (to form the same belief about the case) as the focus-group respondents reached.

Consider an alternative frame for Louise's case:

Louise Logan was driving her SUV down a two-lane rural highway with her baby in the back seat. As she was driving, a sixty-five-foot-long, double-trailer truck pulled out from a field in front of her. Louise was unable to notice the truck in time to avoid it. Experts for both the defense and plaintiff agreed she was moving at fifty-five miles per hour at the time of impact. The force of the collision was enough to knock the seventy-five-thousand-pound truck into the other lane of traffic. Fortunately, the baby was unharmed, but Louise sustained a debilitating fracture of her hip socket, a fractured elbow, and a fractured wrist that required the use of a plate to stabilize it.

It might be tempting to think that this framing is helpful to the plaintiff because it draws attention to the fact that Louise is a young mother with an infant, thereby evoking an empathetic response among jurors. However, focus groups reveal that jurors would likely be suspicious that Louise was not paying attention to the road because she was focused on her baby in the back of the car. Respondents opined that Louise hit the truck because she was looking at the baby. Therefore, this frame leads to jurors creating a story about the case that puts nearly all, if not 100 percent, of the responsibility on Louise.

The best frame, and the one used at trial, is as follows:

> A truck driver was hauling a sixty-five-foot-long, seventy-five-thousand-pound truck out of a farm field onto a two-lane state highway. He says he looked both ways before starting from the field onto the road, but failed to see an oncoming vehicle that was five hundred feet away and clearly in his line of sight. Had he double-checked or scanned the highway at any time after starting to pull out, he would have had five to seven seconds to notice the vehicle and stop short of the highway. During that entire time, his speed never would have exceeded five miles per hour, and he could have stopped in a few feet. But he chose not to continue to scan the highway, and by the time he emerged from the field onto the road, he was going too fast for either driver to avoid a collision. The resulting impact caused Louise Logan, driving her SUV, to suffer a debilitating fracture of her hip socket, a fractured elbow, and a fractured wrist that required the use of a plate to stabilize it.

This frame is all about the truck driver. It forces the jurors to judge the truck driver and discourages them from judging Louise. In the best frame for this case (and most others), the plaintiff is not a central part of the story, at least until the discussion of damages. Getting jurors to focus on the defendant and his conduct makes it much more difficult for the jurors to reach conclusions about or draw on beliefs in the case that are anti-plaintiff. To be sure, the defense will have an opportunity to try to reframe the case, but the plaintiff is far better off if the jurors' starting point is a frame focused on the defendant's conduct. If the jurors are focused on the defendant's conduct, any deeply held beliefs they draw on or beliefs they form about the case will much more likely be about the defendant.

TRIAL LAWYERS' BELIEFS

Jurors are not the only ones with problematic beliefs. Trial lawyers also have beliefs—beliefs that are often different from those of ordinary people. Trial lawyers tend to have heightened sensitivities to injustice—in the same way that an auto mechanic, for example, is more attuned than the general population may be to the way a particular car should drive. Trial lawyers go through three years of formal training and then spend their careers considering questions of justice and liability. The ordinary population does not view the world through that lens. That's why you need to do jury research.

Trial lawyers, for example, tend to view the insurance industry differently than ordinary people do. Many plaintiffs' lawyers see insurance companies as venal profit-mongers seeking to gain at the expense of their insureds. This belief leads many plaintiffs' lawyers to think they should naturally have the upper hand with the jury in an insurance bad-faith case. But focus-group participants have surprised us with their acceptance that insurance companies are in the business of making money by denying claims. Although public opinion data reveals that ordinary people are not fond of insurance companies, they don't generally dislike insurance companies enough to disrupt the status quo by redistributing insurers' assets to aggrieved plaintiffs in bad-faith litigation—unless the plaintiff's trial story includes insurer misconduct that violates jurors' preexisting beliefs.

When you're contemplating beliefs that may be detrimental to your case, it is important to be as mindful of your own beliefs as those of your jurors.

CASE EXAMPLE: OUT-OF-SYNC TRIAL LAWYERS

Cusimano worked with a national team of trial lawyers on a group of cases that highlighted just how out of sync the beliefs of trial lawyers can be from those of the ordinary public. The defendant manufactured printers as well as expensive replacement ink cartridges for those printers, which sold for $35 to $50 each. Opaque and unmarked, the cartridges did not reveal how many ounces of ink they contained. The manufacturer decided to increase profits by cutting in half the amount of ink in the cartridges and charging the same price. The new cartridges weighed the same as the old cartridges, so consumers would not realize that they contained half the ink. Profits soared.

When the practice came to light, it smelled like fraud to Cusimano and a number of other prominent trial lawyers across the country. Multiple law firms banded together and filed suit in more than half the states.

Focus-group respondents in California, however, did not share the trial lawyers' outrage. To them, the covert cartridge swap seemed like a brilliant business decision. Companies are, after all, in business to make money. Meanwhile, Cusimano was busy working up the cases when he learned sometime later of the California focus groups. He conducted his own focus groups, with the same results. It had never occurred to him that jurors would find no fault with the manufacturer's surreptitious scheme for exploiting consumers.

The first cases tried produced a defense verdict, totally consistent with the focus groups. And three of the jurors asked the trial judge if the plaintiffs' lawyers could be turned over to the state bar for ethics violations for filing frivolous lawsuits.

To Cusimano and the other trial lawyers, the switched cartridge practice seemed manifestly unfair—an obvious fraud. But ordinary people shrugged it off. The manufacturer never promised consumers a full ink cartridge. The company was just looking to make more money from a clever business ploy. Let the buyer beware.

WHAT WE HAVE LEARNED

Understand and Apply Beliefs

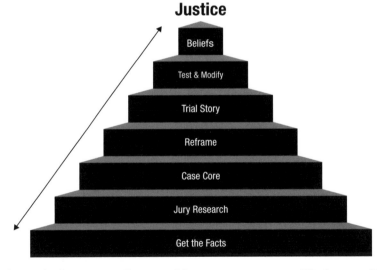

This is the last step in Bottom Up case preparation. Understanding jurors' beliefs and predispositions is about more than just the choice of which battles to pick and which to leave during the course of trial. As you have already read, how you frame your case influences how jurors think about the case, the belief systems they will call on, and the conclusions they will reach. Jurors do not measure and weigh individual facts presented at trial. Rather, jurors get a sense of the whole based on how you present the overall trial story to them. And despite their sworn oath to make no decision until they have seen all the evidence, some jurors will come to conclusions about what happened in the case and decide their own version of the trial story very early in the case opening.

Bottom Up case preparation works in large part because of its emphasis on discovering and understanding jurors' beliefs. Focus groups will help uncover beliefs that may present challenges. Once you're aware of those beliefs, you can develop a trial story that is as consistent as possible with those beliefs. Remember these observations:

- Understand the beliefs jurors will form about your case and how they affect your likelihood of success.
- Isolate both the beliefs that are harmful to your client and the evidence that will lead to beliefs that are harmful to your client.
- Reframe the case if you find yourself in a position where your success hinges on changing jurors' beliefs or likely conclusions about what happened in the case.
- Do not spend time arguing an issue you will lose. Instead, concede the issue and move on to more fruitful ground. Arguing an issue signals to jurors that the issue is important. Do not allow jurors to take cues from you that issues you cannot win are important to the case. Make sure jurors get the message from you that the issues you can win are the issues that are important.
- Make sure you frame your case so the jurors' attention is drawn to the defendant rather than to your plaintiff.
- Finally, don't forget to examine your own beliefs. Trial lawyers don't view the world the way ordinary people do, and it sometimes prevents us from seeing impediments right in front of us.

10

GENUINELY LISTEN AND SPEAK GENUINELY

We've now spent an entire book discussing a process to help you understand a number of interwoven psychological principles that determine how jurors are likely to view your case. We do not believe that there is a better-tested or more effective way to prepare for trial.

But we can't close without mentioning something else we've learned in our own practices. Compelling trial attorneys *genuinely listen and speak genuinely.* To build credibility with your clients and your jurors, practice doing both.

LAW, LAWYERS, AND LISTENING

Have you noticed? No one has time for any real concentration on anything anymore; it is just one interruption after another. "This will only take a minute." Yeah, right. Nothing only takes a minute. Or how about this one? "Could you take a few minutes and look at this brief and tell me what you think? It has to go out this afternoon. It won't take that long, I don't think."

Everyone wants your attention, and they want it now. Your email wants it. The people sending email to you expect you to be there. And they are just waiting for you to respond. They will say they don't really expect you to respond immediately, but if they don't hear from you right away, they will send a follow-up email reminding you that they haven't heard from you. Then, of course, there is the phone. Remember that antiquated device you used to rely on for communication with other human beings before email came on the scene? (And let's not forget texting or social media.)

Trial lawyers—you, the authors of this book, all of us—just don't have time anymore to really concentrate on our cases until we are under the gun, getting ready for trial. Case files often consist of ten to fifteen bankers boxes of papers, which is way too much for any one person to remember. Yet not only must you remember it all, you also have to know exactly what is in each box and why it is important to your client's case.

Before you get too depressed, let us give you some hope. It doesn't have to be this way. Distractions will not go away just because you wish them away. You need to pay attention to the distractions. What are they? When do they affect your work the most?

Listening is the most important part of communication. Think about it. What good is anyone talking, if no one is listening? It's meaningless. The greatest speech in the world is of no value if no one is listening, especially the audience for whom it was prepared. It has been said that "wisdom is the reward for a lifetime of listening."

Many people in relationships don't feel like their partners listen to them. What about the potential clients that come to see you, who are the victims of malpractice? One of the first things they tell you is that the doctors or nurses "just didn't listen to me." Sound familiar? We have had other lawyers' clients call and tell us the exact same thing. They don't think their lawyer is really listening to them.

So, How Do You Win
by Listening?

Start by really listening to your clients. First, treat them like they are important. We would all agree that we aren't much without clients. Bossart likes to show them respect by having his receptionist stand up every time a client comes to the office. She greets them by name and says that he is looking forward to meeting with them. He knows they appreciate it, because they tell him. Acknowledge your clients, and thus listen to their presence in the office.

If you can, keep your office (or a conference room) looking reasonably neat. If you are in the midst of trial preparation, you might have to give it the twenty-three-skidoo cleanup. Have your client's file in the room with clean legal pads for both your paralegal and yourself. If there is an agenda for the meeting, try to stick to it and not interrupt the client at all. If you are prone to interrupting, ask your paralegal to give you a look to clue you in. Constantly remind yourself that this case is about the client, not you. Listening to your client is what it is all about. If this carries through with everyone in the office, you will have a much better chance of getting the information from your client that you need to properly represent them, and you'll know the strengths and weaknesses of their case much earlier.

Listening Skills Are Never Really Taught

Most of us lawyers, especially trial lawyers, see ourselves as much better than average listeners. That is because we have to listen very, very carefully in court and at depositions. We have our listening antennas all the way up, all the time, or we miss a follow-up question we should ask, or get an answer we don't want or like. In truth, however, many times when we read the depositions we have taken, we see where we missed an opportunity to follow up on a question because we weren't listening to the answer the witness gave.

The Skills of a Really Good Listener

Most people are not naturally good listeners. Good listening requires concentration and attention. People who think they can multitask and still be a really good listener are only fooling themselves.

Becoming a good listener requires practice. Most of us are not that good at listening, but once we become aware of the importance of listening and study what it takes to be a good listener, we can develop the skills of a good listener.

The following are skills of every good listener:

◆ A good listener is attentive to the speaker and shows it.
◆ A good listener never interrupts the speaker.
◆ A good listener keeps track of the topic.

- A good listener is sensitive to the speaker's emotions.
- A good listener doesn't jump in at all pauses.
- A good listener respects the value of the speaker's time.
- A good listener, if taking notes, asks the speaker to wait if it's appropriate.
- A good listener asks questions that relate to the speaker's subjects.
- A good listener doesn't leave in the middle of a conversation.
- A good listener invites open discussion.[1]

SIGNS YOU DON'T CARE

There are things people unconsciously do that tell someone that they really don't care about what others are saying. You could say these are rude or perhaps disrespectful behaviors. They will certainly never endear you to someone who is trying to communicate. Avoid these behaviors:

- Not looking at the person talking.
- Looking at your watch.
- Working on the computer while on the phone or while a lecture is going on.
- Not really listening to the answer you get.
- Ignoring a request someone makes during the conversation.
- Not noticing nonverbal responses from another person.

Listening involves far more than just hearing the words the other person is saying. It involves watching the person and trying to understand the emotion of the words he is using. Trial

[1] Larry Barker and Kittie Watson, *Listen Up: How to Improve Relationships, Reduce Stress, and Be More Productive by Using the Power of Listening* (New York: St. Martin's Press, 2000).

lawyers deal with tragic and life-changing circumstances, from the injury or event to the often lasting and terrible consequences. If you are not really listening to your client, you are going to miss the impact, the real trial story, or other details. These details could make a big difference in the case as you present it in settlement or trial.

If it is possible, ask someone else to take notes when you are listening to your client. If you can't find a person, use a digital recorder. Don't take notes yourself. You will miss too much in the communication you are receiving from your client. This is the person who you are asking the jury or insurance carrier to help. Every case must have what Bossart calls a "worthy" client or plaintiff, a person that the average juror is going to want to help. It is the person who comes into the courtroom with clean hands, not begging for help, but deserving help. This is someone who has done what they can to help themselves. The defendant is the one who is not willing to accept responsibility for the injury and who refuses to come forward to help the plaintiff when they should.

Think About What You Are Doing

Tell your paralegal and staff about your new effort in the office to really listen to clients on the phone when they call to give you new information. We all know how important it is to take down information accurately by getting names, phone numbers, and addresses correctly and getting the message the way the speaker intended to deliver it. You need to have the courage to ask your staff how good you are at listening. Then, when they tell you that you aren't listening, you had better face the need to improve your listening skills in your relationships with them.

Think of all the mistakes and misunderstandings that we trial lawyers could eliminate in our offices if we became better listeners. We are responsible for most of the problems. It's time to take action.

In their book *Listen Up,* Larry Barker and Kittie Watson list some of the top ten irritating listening habits.[2] These habits include everything from interrupting the person who is talking to rushing them, getting ahead in an attempt to finish their thoughts, saying things like, "yes, but . . ." as if you've already made up your mind, attempting to top the speaker's statement with a comment like, "That's nothing, let me tell you about . . . ," asking too many questions about the details, or forgetting what you'd previously talked about.

We all do these things, especially in casual conversations with friends. We need to learn how these negative habits affect the person who is trying to communicate with us. This is especially important when communicating with clients. What they are saying is very important to them, and we switch the focus of the conversation to something about us instead of about them.

THE FAILURE TO LISTEN AFFECTS SETTLEMENTS AND TRIALS

Having been a lawyer (and having worked with other lawyers) for over fifty years, Bossart believes that in the past we had time to prepare cases with sufficient thought. However, now we are faced with so many distractions that we have to look

---

[2] Larry Barker and Kittie Watson, *Listen Up.*

much closer at every case to know what it is all about. One of the ways to give more thought to each client's case is to improve your listening skills.

Information is coming at us today at a faster pace than many of us can absorb. At the same time, people have the feeling that no one is listening to them anymore. Patients don't believe doctors are taking the time to listen to their complaints. The result is a wrong diagnosis. Husbands and wives don't have time to talk to each other. Both are working and pass each other like strangers in the night. Parents don't see their kids when they become teenagers. Kids don't feel listened to either. It is a universal feeling. Call your bank (or many other businesses) and you get a recording to push one, two, or three, and then you are on hold for twenty minutes. If someone had listened to you, it would only have taken a minute or two.

We know as plaintiffs' trial lawyers that we must eventually think about our case in earnest in order to put it together for trial or settlement. All too often, we do that in the period closer to trial than we would like to admit. We often listen with the purpose of formulating how we will respond rather than listen with the purpose of understanding. There is always time to respond. By truly listening to the client, the witnesses, the law, the instructions, the experts, and the other side's case, you will have a much better chance of really understanding what the case is about.

WINNING IN TRIAL TODAY

Winning in trial today comes from hard work—putting together an effective trial story, testing that story, and changing it until you are satisfied it gives you the best chance of winning for your client. So, what's new? You have to work a lot harder to win with the jury of today than you did ten to twenty years ago. Juries today are far more suspicious of plaintiffs' trial lawyers than they were before. What satisfied jurors ten to twenty years ago as sufficient proof to win for the plaintiff will not carry the day for today's plaintiff. Today's jurors repeatedly tell us that they have to be almost 100 percent certain, or satisfied to a "moral certainty," that the plaintiff should win before they will decide a verdict for the plaintiff.

WHAT ARE THE RISKS IF YOU DON'T LISTEN?

What are the risks to your cases if you don't listen to your clients and witnesses? The first risk is obvious. You may not win. You may not gain the trust and confidence that you need from your clients to assist you in preparing their cases. In our experience as trial consultants, we often learn critical information that the clients' attorneys did not share because they didn't think it was essential—because it didn't seem necessary for the case's legal proof. It is often only through listening in casual settings, such as over meals, that you will discover the most important piece to your client's case.

How much confidence do you have in a doctor that you turn your health and life over to, who doesn't seem to listen to or care what you tell him? Not much. How many times have you heard clients tell you that they went to see another doctor because the first one "didn't seem to listen to me"?

This work is hard enough without having your own clients not being with you all the way from the beginning through trial. Show your clients from the very first interview that you are willing to listen to them, hear what they say, be concerned about them, and help them with their case. This will go a long way in preventing any feeling that you are not doing what you can to help them win.

WHAT WE HAVE LEARNED

The primary message of this chapter is that we all need to develop the skill of listening in both our work and personal lives. There are a great number of resources available on the subject of how to become a better listener. It is far more than just common sense! You can begin practicing your listening skills right now. Listen in the office and at home. People will notice. Life will be better for you and those around you. Really listen. It will make a difference in the way you communicate and the way others communicate with you.

As Ernest Hemingway said, "When people talk, listen completely. Most people never listen."[3]

And consider what Henry David Thoreau said when he stated, "The greatest compliment that was ever paid me was when one asked me what I thought, and attended to my answer."[4]

---

[3] Malcolm Cowley, "Mister Papa," *Life* 26, no. 2 (January 10, 1949) p. 90.

[4] Henry David Thoreau, *Political Writings*, ed. Nancy L. Rosenblum (Cambridge: Cambridge University Press, 1996), 103.

CONCLUSION

The legendary psychiatrist Dr. Milton Erickson was a communication virtuoso. He revolutionized the field of medical hypnosis and psychotherapy. Erickson taught his students a cardinal rule: to "accept and utilize" the patient's map of the world, as he brings it to the therapeutic relationship.[1] Erickson showed how using the patient's map promoted rapport and trust. He utilized whatever the patient presented to build a bond. In so doing, Erickson communicated he understood and heard the patient. Erickson's teaching served as a guiding light in developing the Jury Bias Model. It was the framework for studying jurors and how they make decisions.

It became clear early in our jury bias research that changing minds was impossible. It was much easier to accept the jurors' tort reform and anti-plaintiff attitudes. "If only jurors were

---

[1] Jeffrey K. Zeig, *The Induction of Hypnosis: An Ericksonian Elicitation Approach* (Phoenix, AZ: Milton H. Erickson Foundation Press, 2014); Jeffrey K. Zeig, ed., *A Teaching Seminar with Milton Erickson* (New York, Brunner-Routledge, 1980); Jay Haley, ed., *Advanced Techniques of Hypnosis and Therapy: Selected Papers of Milton H. Erickson* (New York: Grune & Stratton, 1967).

educated and knew the truth, they would abandon their foolish anti-plaintiff beliefs" was wishful thinking.

Today, it is an accepted fact that exposing jurors to the "truth" about tort reform is useless. Twenty-five years ago, however, we were naive. We were surprised how harsh people were in judging plaintiffs.

The many hours of listening to jurors was eye opening and, at times, jaw dropping. We listened to their concerns. We learned they often felt victimized by lawsuits and the civil justice system. The harm they perceived felt very real to them. It was easier to have a conversation and garner trust by accepting that fact. Attempts to convince them they were wrong elicited resistance and distrust.

We began our jury research as naive realists.[2] We wanted to believe jurors would change their mind about tort reform if they had access to the truth. We expected jurors would approach every case with open minds. We thought we perceived the facts as they were. We thought we were free from bias. We expected the same from jurors. Of course, we were falling prey to naive realism. It is common for people to feel that the reason others do not see it their way is the result of bias. We did not imagine the depth and breadth of anti-plaintiff attitudes we would encounter.

Today, it is an accepted fact that exposing jurors to the "truth" is pointless. Twenty-five years ago, however, we were naive and hopeful about the jury pool. We did not realize that jurors perceived it as an existential threat when we tried to persuade them they were wrong.[3] Asking someone to abandon a belief can be construed as a request to surrender a part of themselves.

---

[2] Lee Ross and Andrew Ward, "Naive Realism in Everyday Life: Implications for Social Conflict and Misunderstanding," (working paper, Stanford Center on Conflict and Negotiation, 1996).

[3] Jonas T. Kaplan, Sarah I. Gimbel, and Sam Harris, "Neural Correlates of Maintaining One's Political Beliefs in the Face of Counterevidence," *Scientific Reports* 6, no. 1 (2016).

Only when we recognized that we needed to accept the juror's map of the world and utilize it did we begin to make progress. Recognizing that Erickson's model was useful in the jury domain was a moment of clarity. Integrating juror attitudes, beliefs, values, and life experiences into the narrative reduces resistance. It also promotes rapport and encourages openness in the case.

The method has scientific support. Jurors search for evidence that supports their attitudes, values, and beliefs. Jurors see it when they believe it. As we've discussed already, decision scientists label this process confirmation bias.[4] Jurors prefer evidence that confirms a preexisting bias even in the face of conflicting scientific evidence. Knowing what jurors need to believe is a priority of pretrial research.

We discovered that once jurors' trial narratives are formed, they are resistant to change. Beliefs about the evidence persevere.

Cognitive scientists describe two types of thinking: an intuitive process and a reflective process.[5] The intuitive process is automatic, fast, and unconscious. The reflective process is conscious, slow, and effortful. Psychologists have named the intuitive process *system one*. The reflective process is *system two*. One psychologist uses a metaphor of an elephant and a rider to describe

---

[4] Charles G. Lord, Lee Ross, and Mark R. Lepper, "Biased Assimilation and Attitude Polarization: The Effects of Prior Theories on Subsequently Considered Evidence," *Journal of Personality and Social Psychology* 37, no. 11 (1979): 2098–2109. (People persist in their beliefs even after the evidence is discredited.)

[5] Daniel Kahneman and Shane Frederick, "Representativeness Revisited: Attribute Substitution in Intuitive Judgment," *Heuristics and Biases: The Psychology of Intuitive Judgment* 49, eds. Thomas Gilovich, Dale Griffin, and Daniel Kahneman (2002); *see also*, Daniel T. Gilbert, "What the Mind's Not," *Dual-Process Theories in Social Psychology* 3, eds. Shelly Chaiken and Yaacov Trope (1999); Keith E. Stanovich, *Who Is Rational?: Studies of Individual Differences in Reasoning* (Taylor & Francis, 1999); Steven A. Sloman, "The Empirical Case for Two Systems of Reasoning," *Psychological Bulletin* 119, no. 3 (1996).

these two systems.[6] The elephant represents system one. System one handles 99 percent of thinking. The rider is system two and is in charge of the other 1 percent of thought.

In jury decision-making, the unconscious and automatic system one predominates. That is not to say that jurors do not use system two to reach a decision. They do, particularly during deliberations when disagreement among jurors is present. However, jurors rely on system one more than system two.

Why should the cognitive system jurors use matter to trial lawyers? Attorneys and their experts rely on system two to develop the trial narrative. Lawyers and experts use an analytical, thoughtful, and reflective process to map the case. Both attorneys and experts use a prism of their profession to think about the case. This creates a translation problem. Lawyers must convert a system-two story into an intuitive, effortless system-one narrative. Otherwise, jurors face immense hurdles. It is like handing jurors the many points of a Seurat painting without informing them about his genius organization in creating the whole.

This book is intended to help lawyers craft simple and elegant system-one narratives. Translating complex facts and issues into digestible chunks of information is hard. Bottom Up case preparation is the process of converting lawyer and expert thinking into juror thinking. That is a fundamental goal of our jury research. The system-one narrative is grounded in the juror's model of the world. Bottom Up case preparation means the following:

- Utilizing the language of juror attitudes, beliefs, and values.
- Telling a story that jurors need to believe about the world.
- Tailoring the trial narrative to make it personally relevant for jurors.
- Translating the system-two arguments and expert opinions into juror language.

---

[6] J. Haidt, *The Righteous Mind: Why Good People Are Divided by Politics and Religion* (London: Allen Lane, 2012).

We know that jurors will use schemas and stereotypes that flow from their life experiences and social norms to evaluate the defendant. Jurors will use these unconscious patterns to make judgments and evaluate when the defendant violated a norm or acted in an unusual manner. Conduct that violates the schemas captures attention. A conflict between the schema and the conduct can serve as a thinking shortcut—a fast and frugal tool for judging behavior.

Evaluating everyday social behavior is easy. Normative behaviors, such as politeness, thoroughness, and empathy, require little effort to evaluate. Deciding whether a doctor breached a standard or if a product is defective requires a complex evaluation. Also, the process of answering such questions can be fraught with ambiguity. It also may require expert knowledge and training. There can be great debate about reasonableness. Jurors prefer easy answers to complex questions. System one converts complex problems into simple ones.

Jurors adopt a system-one narrative early in the trial. Later, jurors will search for system-two arguments to support their story. An expert may opine that a doctor should have used a different surgical approach. Deciding if that expert is right can be difficult. In contrast, it is easy to evaluate whether the amount of time the doctor spent with the patient was sufficient. Again, jurors prefer simple and easy judgments to complex and difficult ones.

In complex cases, like medical negligence, jurors have little experience in evaluating the conduct. Experts may use a complicated, rule-based analysis. Jurors must translate that analysis into a language they understand, such as "the surgeon was in a hurry and did not consider all the information," or "the doctor was cold and callous and did not listen to the patient." Judgments like these are easier. Judgments about medicine are difficult.

System two is a big part of jury decision-making. It legitimizes the jurors' system-one narrative. It helps jurors justify their system-one story. During deliberations, jurors can use system two to explain their judgment. System-two arguments prepare jurors for deliberation. They inoculate them from persuasive appeals from other jurors.

Jurors who are forced to translate system-two arguments into system-one language on their own will turn to anti-plaintiff shortcuts. While jury duty is a physically passive activity, it is exhausting. Using pro-plaintiff shortcuts helps preserve thinking energy and resources. Those shortcuts nudge jurors in the right direction. It makes it easier for jurors to help. A trial lawyer has a huge stake in which shortcuts jurors use. Make the jurors' job easier by providing them with the right energy-saving shortcuts.

Jurors make judgments from small chunks of information. Bottom Up preparation chunks down the facts. Chunking down helps identify facts jurors will overweight. Jurors use the overweighted facts to simplify judgments. Jurors use the over- and underweighted facts as mental shortcuts. Identifying what information jurors overweight is an essential part of Bottom Up jury research.

Consider the following descriptions:

◆ Tina Smith is an eighteen-year-old freshman at Stanford. She was valedictorian of her high school class. Stanford offered her a scholarship for academic excellence. She is premed and hopes to pursue a career in medical research.

◆ Sean Jones is a twenty-year-old sophomore at Berkeley. He was a good student in high school. As a college student, Sean has not been as motivated. He plays the guitar and sings in a local rock band. On weekends, the band plays to student groups and parties.

One night Sean and Tina meet at a party in Palo Alto. Who is more likely to leave the party and drive under the influence of drugs and alcohol, Tina or Sean?

Tina was valedictorian, on scholarship, and premed. Is there a correlation between any of these facts and drinking or doing drugs? Jurors believed there was a negative correlation. These few facts about Tina painted a scenario of an industrious and responsible person.

In contrast, Sean is an unmotivated college student, plays guitar, and sings in a band. Is there a correlation between these facts and drinking or drug use? Jurors believed Sean would be far more likely than Tina to leave the party and drive drunk or while on drugs. The descriptions acted as a priming lens.

Overweighted facts form the framework for the map jurors use to navigate the trial. During voir dire and opening statement, you can make a gift of the map to jurors. The map reduces the amount of energy required to construct a coherent story. It simplifies the jurors' task. It reduces the effort needed to process the evidence. The map gift wraps the case. Providing a map discourages reliance on anti-plaintiff shortcuts. Jurors need a map!

Narrative psychologist Dan McAdams teaches us that "we are the stories we live by."[7] A trial is an act of redemption for the plaintiff. The story of the plaintiff's tragedy, suffered at the hands of another, is a story of redemption. Through acts of personal responsibility and perseverance, the plaintiff transforms a story of suffering into one of redemption. Redemption was a recurring theme in the jury bias research. It is a classic American story.[8]

Despite the dark clouds of the harm, the trial forges a new path for the plaintiff that places the past in the rear-view mirror. In spite of the injuries, the plaintiff remains blessed. He is responsible for his future. When the jurors perceive the plaintiff like this, they are motivated to help. Jurors do not want to help a victim who cannot help himself.

---

[7] D. P. McAdams, *The Stories We Live By: Personal Myths and the Making of the Self* (New York: The Guilford Press, 2006).

[8] D. P. McAdams, *The Redemptive Self: Stories Americans Live By* (Oxford: Oxford University Press, 2013).

Our research shows that empathy moves jurors to help.[9] Jurors need to feel that the plaintiff is hopeful. Only then can jurors believe their actions are worthwhile. Redemption results from the combined forces of the plaintiff and the jury. The future is better for the plaintiff and the community.

That is a central message of the trial narrative. The bond forged between the plaintiff and the jury makes the community a better place. The plaintiff can continue to have a positive impact on self, family, and community. That provides a deeper meaning for the jurors' acts of altruism. The plaintiff and the jury each have a role to play in helping the plaintiff become his best self. The redemption bears fruit in a deeper connection to self, family, and community. Redemption is a hallmark of the story. The trial narrative is deficient without it.

The task of constructing the trial narrative is an empirical process. The process begins and ends with the jurors' map of the world. The empirical method described in this book is essential to winning. This is what Bottom Up case preparation does. It provides a rigorous method through which you can use the Jury Bias Model to create a winning trial narrative. Use it—it works!

---

[9] C. D. Batson, *The Altruism Question: Toward a Social-Psychological Answer* (Hillsdale, NJ: Erlbaum, 1991); C. D. Batson, B. D. Duncan, T. Buckley, and K. Birch, "Is Empathic Emotion a Source of Altruistic Motivation?" *Journal of Personality and Social Psychology* 40, no. 2 (1981): 290–302.

ABOUT THE AUTHORS

David R. Bossart is a plaintiffs' trial lawyer with over fifty years of experience in private practice. He is a nationally known trial consultant for plaintiff trial lawyers and is one of the founding principals of Winning Works, LLC. Bossart has been working with David Wenner and Greg Cusimano on the subject of jury bias for over eighteen years. He collaborates with David Wenner, Greg Cusimano, and Ed Lazarus on working with trial lawyers to help understand the science of decision-making and its practical application.

Bossart is a member of the American Society of Trial Consultants, and has consulted with plaintiff trial lawyers on utilizing the concepts of overcoming jury bias in lawsuits against tobacco, oil, and insurance companies. He has been a fellow in both the American College of Trial Lawyers for over thirty years and the International Academy of Trial Lawyers for over twenty years. Bossart has been designated a Diplomate of Trial Advocacy by AAJ® since 1994, and has also served on AAJ's Board of Governors for twenty-two years. He has lectured nationally for over twenty-five years. David has taught at the National College of Advocacy of AAJ and numerous State TLAs on the subjects of jury selection, overcoming jury bias, case framing, the importance of listening in all aspects of plaintiffs' trial litigation, and personal and professional empowerment (finding balance in life). He has been listed in *Best Lawyers in America* for over thirty years.

Gregory S. Cusimano is an owner in the law firm Cusimano, Roberts & Mills, LLC, in Gadsden, Alabama, where he concentrates his practice on serious personal injury and wrongful death cases. Cusimano, along with David A. Wenner, developed the Jury Bias Model™ that many say revolutionized how cases are tried today, and he continues to conduct research on tort reform rhetoric and juror attitudes. Cusimano is a principal in Winning Works, LLC.

Along with being a frequent speaker at continuing legal education programs throughout the country, Cusimano was a contributing editor of *Alabama Tort Law*, served as coeditor of the six-volume treatise *Litigating Tort Cases*, and developed the award-winning seminar program "Overcoming Juror Bias." He was elected to serve on AAJ's Executive Committee and Budget Committee, was chair of the ATLA (now AAJ) Blue Ribbon Committee to study juror bias, and is a past co-chair of ATLA's National College of Advocacy Board of Trustees. He is a past president of the Alabama Trial Lawyers Association and was named a Fellow of both the American Bar Foundation, the Alabama Bar Foundation, and ABOTA. Listed in *Best Lawyers in America* since 1993, he was awarded the Lifetime Achievement Award by the American Association for Justice, and is a recipient of the Leonard Ring Champion of Justice Award.

Edward H. Lazarus is a partner in the trial strategy firm Winning Works, LLC. In addition to working with lawyers in private practice, Lazarus's clients include political campaigns, bar associations, other professional associations, and political candidates in the US and abroad. Lazarus has done work for ATLA (now AAJ); many state Trial Lawyer Associations; the State Bar Associations of Arizona, Florida, Massachusetts, Nevada, and Hawaii; the state courts in Arizona, Hawaii, Massachusetts, Maryland, and Idaho; and specialty bar associations nationally as well as in more than half of the states in the US and several provinces in Canada.

From 2000 through 2004, Lazarus was the Senior Vice President of State Affairs at ATLA (currently AAJ). In that capacity he assisted state trial lawyer organizations with legislative research, political, legislative, and organizational advice.

In 1994, Lazarus served as Assistant to the Chairman of the Democratic National Committee (DNC) in charge of Strategic

Communications, directing the Research and Communications departments of the DNC. Lazarus developed message strategy for the DNC, and coordinated message and communications strategy among the DNC, the White House, and the House and Senate Democratic leadership.

Lazarus was a founding partner in the political polling and campaign strategy firm Mellman & Lazarus from 1981 through 1993. Among his clients were then US Senator Al Gore; Senate Minority Leader Tom Daschle (SD); Representative Dick Gephardt (MO); Senators Harry Reid (NV), Barbara Boxer (CA), Carl Levin (MI), Ron Wyden (OR), Howard Metzenbaum (OH), John Glenn (OH), and Dan Akaka (HI); as well as many other members of the US House and local elected officials.

David A. Wenner is a partner in the law firm of Snyder & Wenner, P.C. (SnyderWenner.com) in Phoenix, Arizona, and Winning Works, LLC. His law practice is devoted to prosecuting medical negligence and trucking cases. He has obtained numerous multimillion-dollar verdicts and settlements for his clients in Arizona and throughout the United States. He has been listed in *Best Lawyers in America* since 2000.

Wenner has studied juries for the past thirty-five years and is a recognized expert on jury judgment and decision-making. He has published several articles on jury bias, juror and jury decision-making, and trial advocacy. He was co-chair of the ATLA (now AAJ) Blue Ribbon Committee on Jury Bias as well as the AAJ Jury Project. He studied hypnosis and psychotherapy with legendary psychiatrist Milton Erickson, MD, whose work is a theoretical underpinning of the Jury Bias Model™.

Wenner is a frequent lecturer on jury judgment and decision-making and, with Gregory S. Cusimano, developed the Jury Bias Model that is the basis for AAJ's award-winning "Overcoming Jury Bias" college and seminar. The model has been featured in national legal publications and remains one of the only models of trial advocacy grounded in psychological science. Wenner has collaborated on cases with many of the nation's leading law firms.

Before beginning his career as a trial lawyer, Wenner had an active practice of psychotherapy and teaching strategies of psychotherapy to the mental health professional community.